The Right's Road to Serfdom

The Danger of
Conservatism Unbound:
From Hayek to Trump

The Right's Road to Serfdom

The Danger of Conservatism Unbound: From Hayek to Trump

Christopher F. Arndt

Bulkington Press

Cover design, George Foster
Interior design, David Moratto
Bulkington Press
info@bulkingtongroup.com
PO Box 2399
Telluride, CO 81435

First Published 2016

LCCN: 2016916744

ISBN: Hardcover 978-0-9978072-0-2
ISBN: Paperback 978-0-9978072-1-9
ISBN: Ebook 978-0-9978072-2-6

*To the Memory of
My Father Thomas M. Arndt*

Contents

Acknowledgments . . . . *ix*

Introduction . . . . *xi*

1. A Greater Concern with Who Is Governing
   Than with Constraints on Those Who Govern *1*

2. Strong Moral Convictions
   That Trump Political Principles *49*

3. A Lack of Interest in New Ideas
   and Obscurantism When New Ideas
   Appear to Threaten Cherished Values *85*

4. A Tendency toward Imperialism *105*

5. Special Interests
   and Free-Market Fundamentalism *125*

6. The Freedom-Fraud Test:
   #nevertrump, #foreverbachmann? *141*

7. Recovery: Principles Matter *151*

Index *161*

Bibliography *187*

About the Author *201*

Acknowledgments

Without the encouragement, support and guidance from others this book would never have come to fruition. I'd like to thank Richard Ayres for seeing the potential of a book in an essay I shared with him a few years ago — and for encouraging me to write it. At various stages throughout the project, my brothers Channing Arndt, David Arndt, and Michael Arndt, and my mother, Celestine Arndt, also offered important insights and critiques. As a first reader and editor, Charles Babington greatly helped with the precision and clarity of my writing. As a final reader and copy-editor, Julia Perkins further improved the manuscript. Carlin Zia helped with fact checking and references. I owe any improvements in the manuscript to this talented group, and to others who generously offered their time and insights. Any shortcomings and oversights are all my own.

I'd also like to thank my sons Alden and Graham for their patience with their father, their good cheer and their inspiration. Finally, I owe so much to my wife Patty for her enthusiasm and support for me throughout this project and, foremost, for the love, verve, and grace that she brings to my life.

Introduction

From 1940 to 1943, Friedrich Hayek wrote a book entitled *The Road to Serfdom*. The book was dedicated to "The Socialists of All Parties" and it set out in polite and yet painfully clear terms how the socialist vision of a wholly planned and "rational" economy laid the path to National Socialism and Communism. "Few are ready to recognize that the rise of fascism and naziism was not a reaction against the socialist trends of the preceding period but a necessary outcome of those tendencies,"[1] he wrote. The book provided a warning, too, that acting fervently on a simple intellectual error—the belief that a small group of people could direct an entire economy (the "inevitability of planning") —would lead not only to economic demise, but to the loss of political freedom and individual rights. Hayek asked "Is there a greater tragedy imaginable than that, in our endeavor consciously to shape our future in accordance with high ideals, we should in fact unwittingly produce the very opposite of what we have been striving for?"[2]

The irony of recent political developments in the United States is richer still. *The Road to Serfdom* often recounts the observations of socialists in Russia and around the world who were chagrined by the outcome of the sequence of events that they had a role in starting, and yet who did not fully discern the logical connection between those outcomes and their own

---

1. Friedrich A. Hayek, *The Road to Serfdom: A Classic Warning against the Dangers to Freedom Inherent in Social Planning* (Chicago: University of Chicago Press, 1976), 3.

2. Hayek, *The Road to Serfdom*, 5.

beliefs. Typically, those individuals who were more moderately
left of center became isolated: not comfortable with the movement with which they were once identified as it became increasingly radical, but equally out of favor with the "capitalists"
whom they had long considered their opponents. Today, we find
a similar isolation and soul-searching on the American Right.

This earnest soul-searching began during the second Bush
administration. It was not in the foreground of cable news. It
was not spoken of directly by right-of-center politicians. Nor was
it prominently called out by conservative think tanks. Nonetheless, a kind of quiet desperation emerged from some thought
leaders, intellectuals and politicians who had considered themselves to be proud Republicans. These individuals were often
stalwart supporters of Ronald Reagan and Margaret Thatcher,
but the actions of George W. Bush and the Republicans in Congress who supported him gave them pause about the direction
of the Republican Party, and their association with the conservative movement.

Specifically, during the George W. Bush administration,
conservatives seemed to be talking a lot about political freedom,
but acting in direct contradiction to commonly understood
principles of a free society. The problem was not confined to a
single issue.

- Bruce Fein, former Deputy Attorney General under
  Ronald Reagan, was disturbed and astonished by the
  swift demise of the rule of law during the Bush II years.
  "Republicans in Congress have bowed to the president's scorn for the rule of law and craving for secret
  government."[3] Even with appropriate consideration of

---

3. Bruce Fein, "Restrain This White House," *Washington Monthly*, October 2006, http://www.washingtonmonthly.com/features/2006/0610.fein.html.

the security threat posed by Al Qaeda following the September 11 attacks, Fein viewed the expansion of executive power during the Bush II presidency as gratuitous and completely unprecedented. Indeed, George W. Bush had "staked out powers that are a universe beyond any other administration."[4]

- On federal spending, former Republican House Majority leader Dick Armey (1995–2003) was similarly stunned with how poorly his party had fared with basic pocketbook issues while it controlled the presidency and both houses of Congress. "Nowhere was this turn more evident than in the complete collapse of fiscal discipline in the budgeting process,"[5] he wrote in 2006. In a similar way, Bruce Bartlett, who was one of the original supply-siders as a staffer for Jack Kemp, Policy Adviser for Ronald Reagan, and Treasury official for G. H. W. Bush, suggested that the phrase "supply-side economics" had become so abused and perverted that it would be better "to kill the phrase and give it a decent burial."[6]

- On foreign policy, the neoconservative intellectual Francis Fukuyama poignantly recalled a moment when the stark "disjuncture between what I believed and what other neoconservatives seemed to believe"

---

4. Jane Mayer, "The Hidden Power: The Legal Mind behind the White House's War on Terror," *The New Yorker*, July 3, 2006.

5. Dick Armey, "End of the Revolution," *New York Times*, Nov. 9, 2006.

6. Bruce Bartlett, "How Supply-Side Economics Trickled Down," *New York Times*, April 6, 2007, http://www.nytimes.com/2007/04/06/opinion/06bartlett.html?_r=0.

became apparent. By 2006, he would write that the foreign policy school of thought with which he had long identified had "evolved into something that I can no longer support."[7]

- On religious issues, the conservative intellectual Andrew Sullivan was dismayed by the growing influence of religious fundamentalism on the American Right, and the threat this influence posed to political freedom. The temperament of religious fundamentalism had seeped into the party's core. In 2006, he wrote, "Only a deep understanding of the fundamentalist psyche and the theo-conservative project can explain what has happened to the Republicanism in so short a time."[8] Sullivan was also shocked when the Republican Party chose Sarah Palin as its Vice Presidential candidate. He eventually called into question the entire direction of the American Right. "But there has to come a point at which a movement or party so abandons core principles or degenerates into such a rhetorical septic system that you have to take a stand. It seems to me that now is a critical time for more people whose principles lie broadly on the center-right to do so — against the conservative degeneracy in front of us."[9]

7. Francis Fukuyama, *America at the Crossroads: Democracy, Power, and the Neoconservative Legacy* (New Haven: Yale University Press, 2006), xxxi.

8. Andrew Sullivan, *The Conservative Soul: Fundamentalism, Freedom, and the Future of the Right* (New York: HarperCollins Publishers, 2006), 6.

9. Andrew Sullivan, "The Daily Dish: Leaving the Right," *The Atlantic*, December 1, 2009, http://www.theatlantic.com/daily-dish/archive/2009/12/leaving-the-right/193506/.

Some American conservatives, such as David Frum, a former speechwriter for George W. Bush, held out the hope that the direction the American Right had taken under Bush was an aberration, one that would be corrected following the electoral rout in 2008. Others on the Right were less sanguine about the idea of a course correction, given how the Republican base seemed to react to the multitude of failures during the Bush administration. As Senator Lincoln Chafee noted in his 2008 autobiography *Against the Tide*, the personality of George W. Bush seemed to be more important to Bush's supporters than his record of governance.

> Oddly, his pugnacious and intractable attitude remains a big part of his mystique with the Republican core that is still energized as I write this in 2007. Despite his many hollow words and the myriad failures—from Hurricane Katrina to Iraq to peace in the Middle East—the core still loves that President Bush will never back down or change course or admit error. Theirs is the rigid form of thinking that will define the smaller, more aggressive, more extreme Republican Party of the future.[10]

Senator Chafee was correct about the direction of the Republican Party in one important sense: It certainly became more aggressive, more extreme, more focused on the culture, religion, and the personality of leadership than on policy and the task of governance. But the Party did not necessarily become smaller or less effective politically.[11] By 2010, Frum had to accept that

10. Lincoln Chafee, *Against the Tide: How a Compliant Congress Empowered a Reckless President* (New York: Thomas Dunne Books, 2008), 65.

11. Despite a family tradition in Republican politics—his father John Chafee served as governor and senator from Rhode Island as a Republican

the 2008 electoral rout did not lead to the course correction for the Republican Party that he had envisioned. To the contrary, 2010 was a breakout year for the Tea Party and its hardline conservative backers such as Americans for Prosperity. These groups only amplified the anti-compromise, "take no prisoners" attitude of the American Right. The 2010 Republican primary season led to victories for Republican politicians who were more extreme still. "In today's Republican mood," Frum lamented, "politicians who explain practical limits are rejected as weaklings and sell-outs. When [primary candidate] Trey Grayson explains that a Republican majority will not be able to balance the budget in a single year—or that some of the anti-drug programs funded by federal dollars are saving lives—he loses support. When Rand Paul announces that he will never vote for an unbalanced budget, today's angry Republicans hear a man of principle not a petulant grandstander."[12] And, many of the candidates whom Frum had considered to be too extreme to compete in the general election, such as Rand Paul, went on to win.

More disturbing, Frum noted that although conservatives were engaged with elections, they seemed mostly unconcerned with governance.

> I think conservatives do pay attention to elections. What is neglected is governance. How much do we discuss what went wrong with the US economy in the Bush years? If tax cuts are essential to pulling the economy out of recession,

and as Secretary of the Navy under Richard Nixon—Chafee decided he no longer identified with the political party that had been his family tradition, and became a member of the Democratic Party in 2013.

12. David Frum, "Following Rand Paul to Disaster," *FrumForum* (blog), May 13, 2010, http://www.frumforum.com/following-rand-paul-to-disaster/.

why didn't Bush-enacted tax cuts prevent the US economy from tumbling into recession in the first place? Why did incomes stagnate between 2000 and 2007? Why did health cost inflation suddenly accelerate after 2001? What went wrong in the energy markets? How can we do better next time? Interest in these questions varies from slight to negligible. Even our leading think tanks prefer culture war to policy analysis. David Brooks once optimistically hailed a "conservatism of governance." We seem instead to have developed a "conservatism of permanent opposition." If that prospect dismays [conservative commentator] Stacy McCain, as opposition-minded a writer as I know, it should dismay us all.[13]

Fast forward to 2016: Republican soul-searching has moved from the background to the front and center of political debate, from retired/outgoing politicians to politicians in office or actively campaigning, from the blogosphere to Fox News and prominent conservative publications like *National Review.*

Most of this alarm is directed at Donald Trump and the enthusiasm generated by his very successful primary candidacy for the presidential nomination of the Republican Party. But the extent to which many conservatives are surprised and shocked by the success of Trump's primary campaign reflects in part their own denial about the trends long in place in the conservative movement—and the role they may have inadvertently played in Trump's ascent.

To be clear, Trump is unique in important respects. He is cartoonishly vulgar in a way that many other Republican politicians are not. He is self-aggrandizing and self-obsessed, even

13. David Frum, "Bored with Governing," *FrumForum* (blog), August 19, 2010, http://www.frumforum.com/bored-with-governing/.

by politician standards. As a presidential candidate, his lack of experience in government may be unprecedented. Notwithstanding the fact that those characteristics (and others) are cause for legitimate concern, the difficult reality is not the stark break from the conservative movement that he represents, but the continuity.

If nothing else, Trump simply clarifies the growing contradiction that the "Party of Liberty" espouses the virtues of freedom and yet acts otherwise. The key issues that have caused anxiety on the part of prominent politicians and thought leaders on the Right for more than a decade are not exclusive to Trump. If anything, they were amplified across the field of leading Republican primary candidates for the presidency, where we found:

- At best, a lack of concern for civil liberties and the rule of law
- Unserious federal budget plans that point to significant deficit spending
- A lack of concern about melding religion and politics
- An intense focus on the personality of a leader: in particular the mystique of someone who "will never back down or change course or admit error" per Chafee's apt description of Bush II; moreover, the question of who is in charge very much supersedes interest in the task of governance or even the most rudimentary details of proposed policy
- Hostility to science and the expertise of scientists, along with an increasingly troubled relationship with the empirical world

The interesting question is why does the Republican Party—formerly known as the "Party of Liberty"—now have such difficulty with some of the basic principles required for governance in a free society? Many leaders on the Right believe they stand for a free society. But much like the American Left in the early twentieth century, the American Right has unwittingly produced "the very opposite of what it was striving for." How did this happen?

This question is now more relevant than ever because the trends that have been observed in the past decade and a half by the Right's own critics have not necessarily been checked by elections, as many of those critics assumed they would. In 2016, Republicans have 54 of 100 seats in the US Senate and 247 of 435 seats in the House of Representatives. As of March 1, 2016, Republicans control 34 of the 50 state governorships. Fifty-five percent of all state senators and 56% of state representatives are Republican.[14]

To be sure, in the presidential election cycles that occur every four years, Republicans have suffered setbacks in federal offices, but they have not always suffered at the state level. Moreover, the losses at the federal level in presidential elections have often been offset by gains in other election cycles when the presidency was not being contested. Put another way, in 2012 Norman Ornstein and Thomas Mann—two well-respected, nonpartisan political analysts who have each observed the US Congress for more than four decades—offered this sober and now frequently quoted assessment of the Republican Party:

> However awkward it may be for the traditional press and nonpartisan analysts to acknowledge, one of the two major parties, the Republican Party, has become an insurgent outlier—ideologically extreme; contemptuous of the inherited social and economic policy regime; scornful of compromise;

---

14. "Gubernatorial and Legislative Party Control of State Government," Ballotpedia. https://ballotpedia.org/Gubernatorial_and_legislative_party _control_of_state_government.

unpersuaded by conventional understanding of facts, evidence, and science; and dismissive of the legitimacy of its political opposition. When one party moves this far from the center of American politics, it is extremely difficult to enact policies responsive to the country's most pressing challenges.[15]

It is important to note that Ornstein and Mann were making an argument that the Republican Party had become an outlier in terms of their style of politics—what they called "The New Politics of Hostage Taking"—not an argument about political clout. We sometimes assume that the American political system will naturally check extremism, but recent experience over several election cycles suggests this assumption is not necessarily true. Indeed, a political party that controls the legislative branch and 34 of 50 governorships can hardly be considered an outlier from the standpoint of political power.

Regardless of what happens in this year's presidential cycle, the question of why the American Right seems to increasingly stand for a style of politics and an agenda that is at odds with its own rhetoric of political freedom will remain relevant. To answer this question, we need to take a fresh look at the nature of conservatism and its relationship to political freedom.

* * *

Consider that the Founding Fathers of our country were forward-looking inventors, businessmen, architects, lawyers, and scientists. They were men of the Enlightenment. The Constitution

---

15. Thomas E. Mann and Norman J. Ornstein, *It's Even Worse Than It Looks: How the American Constitutional System Collided with the New Politics of Extremism* (New York: Basic Books, 2013), xxiv.

they authored and signed borrowed heavily from the writings of liberals like John Locke. They were respectful of tradition, but held reason and evidence in higher esteem and were open to change—indeed, they welcomed change. Above all, the founders of our constitutional democracy were liberals in the sense that they sought to limit arbitrary authority. The liberal principles embodied in the Constitution were aimed squarely at striking down aristocratic privilege, but those principles also formed a working document such that other arbitrary conventions (slavery, lack of women's suffrage, etc.) could be ultimately changed for a more perfect union.

This book argues that *conservatism unbound tends to run counter to the Enlightenment liberalism that is the basis of our Constitution.* It is better understood as a temperament and a tendency than as a set of principles. It is more clearly seen in Europe where conservatism clings to vestiges of the aristocracy that Americans escaped. To be sure, conservatism can play a legitimate and proper role in opposing drastic change, both abroad and in the United States. But "standing athwart history and yelling stop," as William F. Buckley Jr. famously defined conservatism, is not a political philosophy of freedom. Political conservatism seeks continuity by opposing change, irrespective of principle. By contrast, Enlightenment principles provide the political continuity that enables change. By understanding the nature of conservatism and how it tends against the principles of political freedom, we can understand what has happened to the American Right over the course of the last thirty years.

A Surprising Conservative Critic

Ironically, our task here is greatly aided by Friedrich Hayek himself, who is regarded by many on the Right as a "conservative" hero. Hayek never considered himself a conservative. He called himself a classic liberal, by which he meant an advocate for political freedom in the tradition of Enlightenment liberalism. To Hayek, the conflation of conservatism and the ideas of political freedom posed a danger. He explained this danger, and the differences between the philosophies in an essay, "Why I Am Not a Conservative." This essay is surprisingly relevant today.

The essay, which was first published in 1960, is not well known for two reasons: On the one hand, progressives have neglected Hayek mostly because of his criticism of socialism (the more so because conservatives have exaggerated and mischaracterized his thesis); on the other hand, conservatives have neglected the essay because it exposes the direct contradiction between conservatism and the philosophy of a free society, of which American conservatives believe they are the champions. Conservatives would rather consider Hayek as one of their own —an early stalwart opponent of communism—than as an incisive critic of conservative tendencies.

Hayek argues that conservatism has less in common with classic liberalism than with socialism.[16] He identifies four traits of conservatism that set it in conflict with the classic liberalism/Enlightenment liberalism that he admired. For Hayek, essential and problematic features of conservatism include:

1) A greater concern with who is governing than with the constraints on those who govern
2) Strong moral convictions that trump political principles

---

16. Hayek, *The Road to Serfdom*, xx. By "socialism," Hayek meant the broad movement to *nationalize* industries across the economy. "At the time I wrote, socialism meant unambiguously the nationalization of the means of production and the central economic planning that made this possible and necessary."

3) A lack of interest in new ideas, and obscurantism when new ideas or empirical findings appear to threaten cherished values

4) A tendency toward imperialism

The first four chapters of this book correspond to these four critical points. Hayek's framework enables us to better understand what is going on in American politics and in the Republican Party. More specifically, if one assumes that American conservatives adhere to a philosophy of political liberty, their actions seem inconsistent, indeed, almost bizarre. But if one examines the conservative movement using the rubric outlined above, conservative actions are much more consistent—indeed, they are often predictable in ways that would otherwise not be evident.

Stated differently, it is useful to think about the American Right comprising two different types of "conservatives." One source of confusion is that the Founding Fathers were classic liberals. So classic liberals who want to conserve the political principles of the Founding Fathers often think of themselves as conservatives. On the other hand, there are genuinely temperamental conservatives in Hayek's sense of the word, who are committed to conserving traditional social structures (hierarchies of race, gender, religion, sexuality, culture, etc.). These temperamental conservatives find it convenient to pass as classic liberals, for example appealing to the original intentions of the Founding Fathers whenever it helps them to fight to preserve traditional social hierarchies, but disregarding the liberal principles of the Founders whenever they come in conflict with their conservative vision of society.

Most important, I show in each chapter that the very things conservatives by temperament often promote as political freedom actually undermine political freedom. I call this

misconception—and the promotion of this misconception—
the freedom fraud. In some ways, this tension is plainly evident,
though it has yet to be clearly articulated. For example, a few
political writers have already cited the conservative movement's id (conservative temperament), on the one hand, and
its ego (classic liberalism or "principled conservatism"), on
the other.[17] Fifty years ago, when there were both conservative
Democrats and conservative Republicans, *conservative temperament* was diluted across American politics. Now, as conservatism has become more concentrated and more powerful on the
American Right, what we find is that conservative temperament tends to trump classic liberalism or so-called "principled
conservatism."

It's hard to overstate the effect of this misconception on
American political life. Indeed, the direct, inherent contradiction between the language of liberty that American conservatives like to employ and the conservative tendencies and im-
pulses on which they act sets the stage for a "worst on top"
dynamic for the American Right: those politicians and opinion
leaders who can tolerate, or better yet, promote the contradic-
tion/fraud are rewarded. Conversely, the more consistently and
earnestly one considers the principles required for a free society, the lonelier one tends to be in the GOP today.

* * *

Also in the first four chapters, we take a close look at the most
distilled and potent version of the freedom fraud: the simplistic

17. Ezra Klein, "Donald Trump's Victory Proves Republican Voters
Want Resentful Nationalism, Not Principled Conservatism," *Vox* (blog),
May 4, 2016, http://www.vox.com/2016/5/4/11586360/donald-trump-
conservatism

idea that "the best government is the least government." This phrase is sometimes attributed to Ronald Reagan's first inaugural address. What he actually said in that speech was: "In this present crisis, government is not the solution to our problem; government is the problem."

Clearly, the case that he made in the speech was against a specific set of conditions where he thought the federal government was overreaching to the point of being a burden, and not a benefit. However, he explicitly did not say that the federal government was *always* a burden. To make this point perfectly clear, a few sentences later, in the very same speech, he stated: "Now, so there will be no misunderstanding, it's not my intention to do away with government. It is rather to make it work —work with us, not over us; to stand by our side, not ride on our back. Government can and must provide opportunity, not smother it; foster productivity, not stifle it."[18]

Both of Reagan's statements in the speech are eminently reasonable—consistent, too, with principles of liberty. But conservatism has a tendency to convert the reasonable notion that it is possible for the federal government to overreach to a kind of simplistic, fundamentalist sentiment that government is always the problem and "the best government is the least government."[19] Consider Rick Perry's famous gaffe during the

---

18. Ronald Reagan, "Inaugural Address," Washington, DC, January 20, 1981.

19. Henry David Thoreau, *Resistance to Civil Government*, Webtext created by Jessica Gordon and Ann Woodlief, Virginia Commonwealth University, 1999, http://transcendentalism-legacy.tamu.edu/authors/thoreau/civil/ To be clear, the notion that freedom is simply the lack of government predates Ronald Reagan. Thoreau gave this view its classic expression in the very first sentences of his essay *Resistance to Civil Government*: "I heartily accept the motto, — 'That government is best

2011 Republican primary debate. The debate will always be known for Perry's inability to remember the third agency he wanted to eliminate (the Department of Energy). More remarkable was what he was actually proposing: eliminating the Commerce Department, for example.

The Commerce Department houses the US Patent and Trademark Office, which oversees our system of intellectual property, granting patents and trademarks as set forth by Article I of the US Constitution. The purpose of patents and trademarks is "To promote the progress of science and useful arts, by securing for limited times to authors and inventors the exclusive right to their respective writings and discoveries." The Commerce Department also includes the Census Bureau, which fulfills another Article I constitutional requirement: carrying out the decennial census. The accurate count of Americans that the department provides each decade lets leaders and policymakers know how to allocate resources—housing, roads, utilities—around the country. It helps determine the very make-up of congressional districts. Beyond the Patent Office and the Census Bureau, other important functions, such as collecting economic data and setting industrial standards, are a part of the Department of Commerce. For all this, note

---

which governs least;' and I should like to see it acted up to more rapidly and systematically. Carried out, it finally amounts to this, which I also believe,—'That government is best which governs not at all'..." And, there are surely backwoods Thoreau-type anarchists on the political Right and the Left. But in modern American politics, the consequential strain of "the best government is the least government" is most often associated with conservatism and the political Right. Moreover, focusing on Reagan's inaugural address is appropriate because, content notwithstanding, it marked the beginning of a period in which this idea of political freedom became more broadly accepted.

that the Commerce Department accounts for about 0.2% of the US federal budget, or about 0.005% of the US economy.

What Perry proposed at the debate was to strike a direct blow at the US Constitution and arguably the innovation engine of the American market economy. Was this proposal ridiculed as directly at odds with a market economy and a free society? Penny wise and pound foolish? To the contrary, the proposal did not evoke a serious discussion on the Right—in the debate or afterward.[20]

Moreover, the logic of the freedom fraud is often tacitly accepted in our broad political discussion. For example, debate over the role of government today is commonly framed by the question of "more" versus "less" government with little consideration for what the government is doing. The crude implicit assumption is that political freedom corresponds to a simple kind of volume button of government activity: turn government up, you get less freedom, turn government down, and you get more freedom. This framework is completely ingrained in the way we think about public policy issues, despite the obvious fact that we need government to secure liberty.

Acknowledging that there are positive requirements on the part of government for a free society enables us to start thinking again about where government actions promote liberty, what actions are essentially neutral with regard to political freedom, and what actions impair liberty. For example, political freedom is often greatly impaired when government *fails to act*

---

20. If pushed, the Perry campaign would almost surely state that their intention was not to eliminate the Patent Office and other critical functions, but to relocate them into other agencies and therefore streamline government. However, "streamlining government" is never mentioned explicitly because it requires the recognition that our government does provide critical functions required for a free society.

—when it fails to enforce property rights, establish independent courts, enforce laws, regulate money and banking, deter fraud, reduce pollution (a corruption of property), define intellectual property, establish standards such as weights and measures or Internet protocol, and provide a taxation function that is deemed fair and equitable. These functions are among essential prerequisites for which we need a vital and active government to promote a free society.

Today, these essential functions are often ignored, underfunded, or even directly attacked in the name of liberty. This indiscriminate (and ultimately nihilistic) rant to "roll back government" is rarely countered effectively on grounds of principle. Allowing the misguided concept that "the best government is the least government" to fester on its own relates directly to Frum's earlier observation that the conservative movement's interest in governance varies "from slight to negligible." There is no reason to be interested in governance, policy, or political principles if a one-phrase ideology already provides the answer to all.

* * *

Finally, in chapters 5 to 7, I offer some insight as to why we are susceptible to the freedom fraud and how we can begin to recover. In chapter 5, I examine why special interests are a natural beneficiary of the freedom fraud and an eager partner in its promotion. Much has been written about how money and special interests are corrupting our politics and political principles. But very little has been written about how a corrupt notion of freedom enables money and special-interest influence. In chapter 6, I argue that the first step in reversing the destructive influence of the freedom fraud is to have a method to identify it easily. Toward this end, I propose a "freedom-fraud" test.

The last chapter offers a framework to help us move beyond

the freedom fraud. This framework shows that many of the most important requirements of a free society in terms of government are among the least costly to fund. We can start to move beyond the freedom fraud by forging a consensus on the need for vibrant, active, and effective government that supports these functions. For the tasks of government that require a larger footprint, we can also locate a sphere of federal activity where we can at least agree to disagree.

One might ask, why do we need a framework to think about government and a free society? Don't we already have the Constitution? Yes, but we also often carry in our minds an even more simplistic notion of freedom—"the best government is the least government"—that leads to confusion and inconsistent actions that often directly undermine the Constitution (for example, eliminating the Commerce Department). Captivated by the freedom fraud, we drift—away from a debate over the laws, policies, evidence, science, and principles that enable us to solve practical problems as they arise—to the cult of personality, religion, suspicion, and fear as the basis for government. In short, there is strong connective tissue from "the best government is the least government" to Perry's inane proposal to eliminate the Department of Commerce and to the successful primary candidacy of Donald Trump, where governance as it relates to a free society does not seem to matter at all.

Chapter 1

A Greater Concern with Who Is Governing Than with Constraints on Those Who Govern

In general, it can probably be said that the conservative does not object to coercion or arbitrary power so long as it is used for what he regards as the right purposes. He believes that if government is in the hands of decent men, it ought not be too much restricted by rigid rules. ... Like the socialist, he is less concerned with the problem of how the powers of government should be limited than with that of who wields them; and, like the socialist, he regards himself as entitled to force the value he holds on other people. —F. A. Hayek

Hayek's insight that conservatives tend to care foremost about who is governing helps us understand actions and priorities that otherwise seem at odds with a political philosophy of freedom. Focusing chiefly on the type of person in charge, conservatives are indifferent or even averse to constraints or "rigid rules" that limit the powers of those in government whom they trust.

From this standpoint, we can more easily see why confusion arises over conservatives' true and proven commitment to freedom. It is not just that the conservative temperament is something other than the political philosophy of freedom, but it tends against the principle of restraint in a very direct sense (for more explanation on this point, see "Addendum: A Refresher on Restraint and Political Freedom" at the end of this chapter).

In this chapter, we examine two areas where conservative

actions belie their professed commitment to freedom. We first look at the Republican record of federal spending, and the riddle of why "supply-side economics" has such enduring appeal for the conservative movement. Then we examine the conservative response to security threats—which at times seems to treat the rule of law itself as central to the problem—particularly international laws and treaties.

Why Conservatives Are Big Spenders

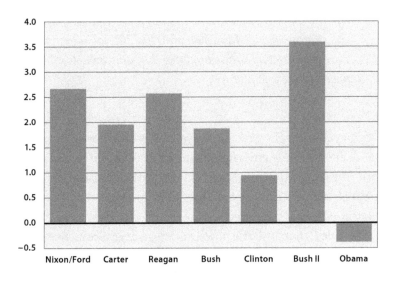

The insight that conservatives care much more about who is governing than about the constraints on those who govern greatly helps our understanding of why Republicans have been big spenders at the federal level. The chart above, which shows the per-capita growth rate of total government expenditure in real terms, lays out the numbers in clear detail.[1]

1. Total government expenditures include consumption expenditures plus other activities, such as gross investment and transfer payments (US

In the past 45 years during the periods in which the party of so-called "limited government" has held the presidency, government spending has grown consistently faster than when the so-called "tax and spend" liberals have held the office. In addition, the general pattern is not only a faster rate of spending during GOP administrations, but also spending that exceeds tax receipts and other revenues and therefore is financed by debt. The chart below shows the federal government's deficit or surplus over the same period from the start of the Nixon administration to the present. The pattern is unmistakable. The federal deficit increases during Republican administrations (arrows down) and stays flat or is reduced during Democratic administrations (arrows horizontal or sloping up).

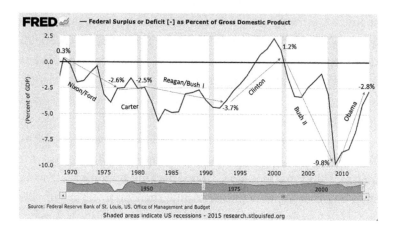

Bureau of Economic Analysis (BEA) National Income and Product Accounts (NIPA) Table 3.1. Expenditures are deflated to 2009 dollars using the personal consumption expenditures chained price index (BEA NIPA Table 1.1.4), and converted to per capita terms using mid-period total population (BEA NIPA Table 7.1). Annualized growth rates are calculated from the inaugural quarter of each presidential term through the inaugural quarter of the succeeding presidency (i.e., Q1–Q1), except Obama, which uses Q1 2016 as an end point since his full term in office is not complete.

To the extent that this comes as a surprise, it reflects not just a conservative movement that is at odds with its rhetoric, but a press and an entire political community that, on the whole, is only vaguely aware of underlying economic trends. The accepted narrative that the conservative party cares foremost about freedom and reducing the size of government is so thoroughly ensconced in the minds of most people who follow politics that it is difficult to comprehend facts that show otherwise. If anything, the facts suggest a narrative of "tax-cut and spend conservatives" followed by "tax and expense-cutting liberals." What's going on?

For a political conservative, matching revenue to expenses is not a must-have. Their hearts are in other places. They like spending that supports their values or power, such as military spending, farm subsidies, and more recently Medicare/Social Security—together about 59% of federal spending—although they often give lip service to reining in those programs. What irritates conservatives is federal spending on items like science, family planning, and foreign aid (together about 3% of federal spending).

We see this in almost every Republican primary presidential debate. The total dollars matter much less than the symbolism. What matters more than anything to conservatives is spending that appears to undermine their own culture or values. *That* is spending to oppose. But if a conservative is in power, spending is viewed in an entirely different light. Spending per se is not the issue: *who is spending the money and for what purpose matters most.* As Hayek points out in the quote that opens this chapter, the ethos of a political conservative is that "if government is in the hands of decent men, it ought not be too much restricted by rigid rules." This dynamic explains why the conservative movement shifts from a more passing, nominal interest in deficit-reduction and debt when it holds power to deficit-mania-inspired government shutdowns and debt-default threats when Democrats hold power.

In short, the same impulse that leads conservatives to ignore constraints when they are in power drives them to try to impose constraints when others are in power. What makes a political principle, such as fiscal restraint, a principle, is that it is evenly applied. Despite talk, conservatives don't value the principle of fiscal restraint in general. Indeed, as the GOP has become increasingly conservative, the notion that Republicans are the party of fiscal constraint has become increasingly suspect.

The History of PAYGO is Telling

The history of the budgetary rule PAYGO (Pay As You GO) provides a vivid illustration. In general, PAYGO requires all increases in direct spending or revenue decreases to be offset by other spending decreases or revenue increases. Therefore, the rule makes it difficult to launch new spending programs without financing them with new taxes or finding an offsetting program to cut. Conversely, the rule makes it difficult to cut taxes without cutting spending somewhere in equal measure. The initial purpose of the rule was to restrain Congress from deficit spending. The inspiration for setting the rule came on the heels of significant deficit spending during the Reagan Administration and the first part of the George H. W. Bush administration.

When PAYGO was initially adopted under the first Bush as part of the Omnibus Budget Reconciliation Act of 1990, conservatives saw betrayal and disaster. Not only did the first Bush go back on his pre-election promise of "no new taxes," but PAYGO logic directly contradicted the hardening supply-side dogma, which conveniently provided a justification for conservatives to cut taxes without cutting spending. When Bill Clinton took office, however, interest in removing the restraining measure vanished. It was extended in the Omnibus Budget Reconciliation Act of 1993 and the Balanced Budget Act of 1997. For conservatives, it is all well and good to restrain spending under a Democratic president.

But, unsurprisingly, after George W. Bush assumed office in January of 2001, PAYGO expired and it was not long until a Republican-controlled Congress, with George W. Bush's strong support, quickly ramped up deficit spending. Fending off criticism from moderates and deficit hawks, Vice President Dick Cheney asserted that "Reagan proved that deficits don't matter." Even John Maynard Keynes, regarded on the far Right as a kind of grandfather of inflationary deficit spending, was invoked by conservatives as a rationale for the stimulus-promoting Jobs and Growth Tax Relief Reconciliation Act of 2003. Furthermore, it is not as if Republicans during the George W. Bush era were not given the chance to reinstate PAYGO and govern with fiscal constraints. By 2004, the economy was recovering from the dot com bust and Republicans were offered a chance by Democrats to bring back PAYGO rules in what Jonathan Chait called

a deal a spending hawk ought to have leapt at. Here was an unimpeachably effective tool to keep Congress from launching the spending binges conservatives so disdain. The only price was making tax cuts harder to enact. The Republican reaction to this offer was telling. Conservative pundits denounced it unanimously, and the GOP Congress buried it. As House Majority Leader Tom DeLay said at the time, the "pay as you go" requirement was "contrary to our fundamental beliefs."[2]

To recap PAYGO, it was adopted in 1990 during the first Bush administration, but with intense opposition from the Republican Party's conservative wing. It was reaffirmed under Bill Clinton. Finally, it was abandoned under George W. Bush, and specifically shunned again in 2004 when Republicans controlled both houses of Congress as well as the Presidency. It is telling that the 2000–2006 period, when conservatives consolidated power by controlling the executive branch and Congress, marked a dire turn toward fiscal irresponsibility.

The aftermath of the 2006 election, when Republicans lost both houses of Congress, brought about some reflection on Republican spending excesses. Two days after the election, a chagrined former Republican House Majority leader Dick Armey (1995–2003) painfully noted the large chasm between Republican actions and the conservative narrative of small government and freedom that is sold to the public.

Nowhere was this turn more evident than in the complete collapse of fiscal discipline in the budgeting process. For most Republican candidates, fiscal responsibility is our political bread and butter. No matter how voters view other, more divisive issues from abortion to stem-cell research, Republicans have traditionally enjoyed a clear advantage with a majority of Americans on basic pocketbook issues. "We will spend your money carefully and we will keep

---

2. Jonathan Chait, *The Big Con: The True Story of How Washington Got Hoodwinked and Hijacked by Crackpot Economics* (Boston: Houghton Mifflin Company, 2007), 108.

your taxes low." That was our commitment. This year, no incumbent Republican (even those who fought for restraint) could credibly make that claim. The national vision —less government and lower taxes—was replaced with what Jack Abramoff infamously called his "favor factory." One Republican leader actually defended a questionable appropriation of taxpayer dollars, saying it was a reasonable price to pay for holding a Republican seat. What was most remarkable was not even the admission itself, but that it was acknowledged so openly. Wasn't that the attitude we were fighting against in 1994?[3]

The Hayek quote that begins this section predicts the outcome that Armey describes. The party's weak ego for restraining government was predictably overwhelmed by its conservative id that favors having the "right people in charge."

Contemplating the same collapse in Republican fiscal discipline at about the same time as Armey, Chait raises a question that he himself cannot seem to answer.

The perplexing question is why the spending hawks never question their subservient place in the Republican coalition. After all, their party's reigning ideology inevitably fails to shrink government, and demonizes an alternative path (make deals with moderate Democrats to raise taxes and cut spending) that has proven to succeed. But, while they may incessantly bemoan their party's failure to cut spending, they never question the underlying priorities that produce this failure.[4]

3. Armey, "End of the Revolution."

4. Chait, *The Big Con*, 108.

Despite very different vantage points on the political spectrum, Chait and Armey are misled by the same common misperception of conservatism, which is that conservatives in general have strong political principles, with fiscal constraint being paramount. With that assumption unshaken, Armey portrays the situation as a kind of dramatic tragedy where those who come to power turn their back on the very thing for which they stand.

In a similar fashion, Chait fails to fully appreciate the natural tension between fiscal constraint and conservative tendencies. He therefore characterizes the dominance of supply-side economics on the Right as a triumph achieved by a small elite essentially hoodwinking the entirety of an unwilling conservative base. To be clear, Chait's book is generally terrific as it provides a detailed and incisive account of what is in fact a relatively small group of supply-side zealots who have been extraordinarily influential in setting US economic policy.

What Chait fails to fully appreciate (and what I will discuss at the end of this section) is the way in which supply-side economic theory dovetails with conservative temperament. The enduring power of supply-side theory owes as much to elite zealotry as to the manner in which it resonates with the base. For both Chait and Armey, the crucial oversight is the fact that conservative temperament trumps and indeed runs exactly counter to the rhetoric of political freedom that conservatives employ.

Why Conservatives Need Supply-Side Economics

Once one understands the opposing tension between conservatives' language of freedom and conservative temperament, one is in a much better position to understand the enduring power of supply-side economic theory. To be sure, it is more accurate to think about supply-side theory coming in two versions: a modest, debatably true theory that is mostly ignored; and an extreme, implausible theory that has been frequently put into practice, demonstrably proven false, but nonetheless has become reigning dogma for the conservative movement.

Both versions of supply-side theory begin with the self-evident observation that a tax rate of zero will lead to no government revenue. Conversely, if the government taxes at a rate of 100%, it is not likely to collect any revenue either—what's the point of working if the government is simply going to take all your money? The arc of the line that connects those two points on an x-y plot is the so-called Laffer Curve, after the supply-side economist Arthur Laffer. In between the extreme tax rates of 0% and 100% there is a place—by definition—where if you lower taxes, you would get more revenue. For example, moving from a tax rate of 100% to a tax rate of 90% would motivate some people to work as opposed to no people working, and therefore the government would collect some revenue.

The modest and sane version of supply-side theory holds that in some real-world circumstances, a reduction in a tax rate could boost economic activity and thereby lead to an increase in government revenue. The most likely circumstance would involve a rate reduction from a very high marginal tax rate, where the change in the tax rate results in a very large change in the incentive to work. This incentive change would encourage more economic activity than would be the case with the older, higher rate structure—and possibly more overall tax revenue.

Whereas the modest version of the supply-side theory pays close attention to incentives, the extreme version casts all that aside and blithely asserts that virtually any reduction in a tax rate from almost any level will always result in more revenue to the government. Period. On the face of it, the extreme theory is as dogmatic as it is highly implausible.[5] This theory argues that increased economic activity resulting from a lower tax rate will

---

5. Martin Feldstein, interview by Douglas Clement, *The Region*, July 10, 2006, posted by Mark Thoma, *Economist's View*, Sept. 20, 2006, http://economistsview.typepad.com/economistsview/2006/09/an_interview_wi.html. The same logic that supports supply-side theory on the benefit of reducing very high marginal tax rates works in reverse for a reduction in a tax rate that starts from a comparatively low threshold. For example, if a tax rate is lowered from a marginal rate of 90% to 80% the amount of money the taxpayer gets to keep doubles from $0.10 to $0.20—that's a big incentive! It is plausible that such a large change in the incentive to work could lead to more economic activity. But as one moves farther away from a 100% marginal tax rate, the incentive change is reduced dramatically at a nonlinear rate. For example, the "same" ten-percentage-point reduction in the tax rate from 20% to 10% results in only a 12.5% increase in take-home pay for every marginal dollar earned (the change from $0.80 to $0.90). Increasing your take-home pay by 12.5% is a very different incentive from increasing it by 100%. Moreover, the math on revenue-collection for the government is the reverse. The tax-rate reduction from 90% to 80% results in a huge change to the incentive to work, but a fairly modest immediate percentage loss of revenue to the government of 11% (this is the loss prior to considering any boost to economic activity). On the flip side, the tax rate reduction from 20% to 10% results in a very modest change to the incentive to work, but a monumental immediate percentage loss of government revenue of 50%.

For this reason, the modest version of supply-side theory posits that a reduction in tax rates will typically result in *revenue loss*, but not exactly on a dollar-for-dollar basis. So, a ten-percentage-point decline in a marginal tax rate from 30% to 20% would result in a large decline in government revenue, but some of the loss would be made up for by the increase in the incentive to work. For example, Feldstein has suggested the loss in government revenue would be approximately 2/3 of what the static loss would project.

always overcome the loss of revenue caused by the newly lowered rate. Starting from more normal tax rate levels—and in particular as tax rates get pushed lower and lower—that theory has been disproven time and again.

To this simplistic and demonstrably false concept, the extreme version of supply-side theory adds a political economy corollary whose logic is more specious still: Tax cuts will result in less government by eventually forcing the government to make spending cuts, the so-called "starving the beast" or "cutting the government's allowance" theory. It's very difficult to comment on this theory without coming off as snarky, but Chait probably sums it up best, noting that it is

> remarkable how many conservatives take seriously such an obviously witless analogy. Cutting the government's "allowance" does not limit its capacity to spend. The proper analogy would be reducing your child's allowance but giving him unlimited use of your credit card.[6]

Not a single reputable economist takes the extreme version of supply-side economic theory seriously. Of course, there are economists who are proponents of the modest version of supply-side economic theory. And, with varying degrees of effort and enthusiasm, they labor to walk back the extraordinary claims of extreme supply-side theory. Sometimes this effort is made while also accusing supply-side critics of creating a straw man and of unfair criticism of an otherwise constructive approach. The problem is that the modest version of supply-side theory is mostly ignored while the extreme version of the supply-side theory is ceaselessly promoted by right-wing think thanks and editorial boards of publications such as the *Wall*

6. Chait, *The Big Con*, 106.

Street Journal and *National Review.* Ultimately, it is the extreme version that has become gospel among right-wing politicians and adopted as policy.

In 2007, Bruce Bartlett, who was one of the original supply-siders as a staffer for Jack Kemp, a policy adviser for Ronald Reagan, and a Treasury official for George H. W. Bush, described the situation like this:

> But today it is common to hear tax cutters claim, implausibly, that *all* tax cuts raise revenue. Last year, President Bush said, "You cut taxes and the tax revenues increase." Senator John McCain told National Review magazine last month that "tax cuts, starting with Kennedy, as we all know, increase revenues." Last week, Steve Forbes endorsed Rudolph Giuliani for the White House, saying, "He's seen the results of supply-side economics firsthand— higher revenues from lower taxes."[7]

A chagrined Bartlett went on to state that because supply-side theory was being used to support the "most gimmicky, economically dubious tax cuts with the same intensity," that perhaps the best thing to do would be "kill the phrase 'supply side economics' and give it a decent burial." But killing the supply-side theory is tricky. The challenge is that supply-side theory as practiced is really less about an economic theory than it is about the contradictions inherent in American conservatism. There is a reason the extreme version of supply-side theory has become dominant as the Republican Party has become more stridently conservative.

Conservatives face a practical problem; supply-side theory elegantly addresses it. Although they nominally profess to be in

---

7. Bartlett, "How Supply Side Economics Trickled Down."

favor of liberty and accountable government, they don't want to be subject to fiscal constraints. The fiscal hawk who holds the position that "deficit spending is taxation deferred" stands as an impediment to those conservatives in power longing to do what they please. With supply-side theory, they can pretend they will magically do both. They can govern without spending constraints and somehow advance small-government "liberty" at the same time. In short, the theory is an elegant fantasy that bridges the stark contradiction between classic liberalism and conservatism.

The fact that the extreme version of supply-side theory serves this critical function for conservatives explains the theory's durability despite the absence of academic support and decades of evidence to the contrary. For a moment, the lone exception that proved the rule was a 2010 article in *National Review*, one of the high priesthoods of conservative thought. In the article, "Goodbye, Supply Side," author Kevin Williamson stepped well beyond conservative orthodoxy and stated the obvious failure of supply-side economic theory:

> Despite all those pro-growth tax cuts, our deficits continue to grow faster than our economy. That's been especially true during the Great Recession, but even during periods of strong economic growth, there has been nothing to indicate that our economy is going to grow so fast that it will surmount our deficits and debt without serious spending restraint. This should be a shrieking klaxon of alarm for conservatives still falling for happy talk about pro-growth tax cuts and strategic Laffer Curve optimizing. Tax cuts aren't really the problem. The hot action is on the spending side of the ledger, and nobody wants to touch it. The problem with magical supply-siderism is that it gives Republicans a rhetorical and intellectual framework in

which to ignore spending— just keep cutting taxes, the argument goes, and somebody else will eventually have to cut spending. The results speak for themselves: Tom DeLay and Dennis Hastert and Trent Lott and Bill Frist all know how to count, but, under their leadership, Republicans spent all the money the country had and then some. Deficits boomed, and Republicans' claim to being the responsible britches-wearing adults when it comes to spending got unpantsed. Cutting taxes is easy. Cutting spending is hard.[8]

In a blog post shortly after the above article was published, Chait described Williamson's piece as the "GOP's Secret Speech" in a reference to Khrushchev's 1956 speech denouncing Stalin's cult of personality. At the time, Chait held no illusions about how long it would take to undo 35 years of supply-side dogma, but he nonetheless called the article "a pretty remarkable first step" with the implication that this might be the beginning of the end of supply-side theory, if not the end.[9]

Alas, even the guarded Chait may have been too optimistic. One passage from the article should have given him pause: "Spending cuts are always popular in theory and detested in practice," Williamson wrote, "but the deficit is now truly terrifying, and, fortunately for Republicans, it is owned by Barack Obama and Nancy Pelosi." Translation: *Since voters erroneously associate the current fiscal disaster with Barack Obama and*

---

8. Kevin Williamson, "Goodbye Supply Side," *National Review*, May 3, 2010, http://www.nationalreview.com/article/229574/goodbye-supply-side-kevin-d-williamson.

9. Jonathan Chait, "The GOP's Secret Speech," *New Republic*, May 4, 2010, http://www.newrepublic.com/blog/jonathan-chait/the-gops-secret-speech.

Nancy Pelosi, we might as well stop pretending that tax cuts reduce the size of government and actually focus on spending cuts because the Democrats will bear the political pain. The timing and pure expediency of the argument should have provided pause as to whether Williamson's article was a turning point portending the demise of supply-side dogma or simply a temporary reprieve before conservatives returned to their normal "tax cut and spend" ways.

Looming: Supply-Side Spending with Unparalleled Force

The more conservative the Republican party becomes, the more it needs supply-side theory to bridge the chasm between the way it wants to wield power and the misplaced rhetoric of freedom. This insight helps explain our current situation. Neither the full weight of past supply-side historic failures, nor even a surprisingly frank admission of those failures in an iconic conservative publication has slowed supply-side momentum. In terms of the 2016 Republican presidential primaries, the extreme version of supply-side economics not only came back, but came back with unprecedented, blanket support. The exuberantly warm reception by Republican politicians of supply-side theory was telegraphed in a spring 2015 article in the *Washington Post*: "Arthur Laffer Has a Never-Ending Supply of Supply-Side Plans for GOP."

> As the 2016 GOP primary season takes off, Laffer is more in demand than ever before, with Republican candidates embracing tax-cut-for-the-rich policies even as they bemoan economic inequality. Candidates have been meeting with him in recent weeks, and on Friday in Nashville, he says, his schedule includes Rick Perry at 10 a.m., Ben

Carson at noon, Jeb Bush at 1:15 p.m. and Bobby Jindal at 5. Dinner is scheduled with Ted Cruz. He has already met at least once with Wisconsin Gov. Scott Walker.[10]

And sure enough, the early Republican primary season (summer–fall of 2015) was a kind of fiscal twilight zone for the conservative movement. The fever pitch of deficit-reduction mania, quite useful for derailing Barack Obama's legislative agenda, now overlaps with a fever pitch of supply-side deficit creation as Republicans seek the Presidency. The process whereby conservative candidates have unveiled their tax plans to the public has taken the form of a kind of race to the bottom of fiscal irresponsibility. The political reporter Jordan Weissmann correctly captured the dynamic whereby the least responsible plan from the standpoint of the federal deficit is embraced:

> Without factoring in growth, [the conservative Tax Foundation] found that Trump's plan would actually add $11.98 trillion to the 10-year deficit. Once the boost to growth that would result from slashing taxes is factored in, it would only cost $10.14 trillion ... more or less cratering the government's finances into fiery rubble. Theoretically, this should be problematic for Trump, who claims his proposal wouldn't add to the debt or deficit. But the funny thing is, I actually think he'll run with this. Because his cuts are so, *so* huge, the Tax Foundation—which has great faith in the ability of tax reductions to spur the economy—says the

-----

10. Jim Tankersley, "Arthur Laffer Has a Never-Ending Supply of Supply-Side Plans for GOP," *Washington Post*, April 9, 2015, https://www. washingtonpost.com/business/economy/arthur-laffer-has-a-neverending-supply-of-supply-side-plans-for-gop/2015/04/09/04c61440-dec1-11e4-a1b8-2ed88bc190d2_story.html.

plan will create 5.3 million extra jobs over 10 years. Jeb Bush's own deficit-ballooning tax proposal—which Trump seems to have more or less grabbed, then doctored a bit by slashing rates further—would add a mere 2.7 million jobs, according to the think tank's math. Marco Rubio's preferred tax cuts, which once seemed completely laughable in their own right but appear almost quaint compared with the Donald's, would add just 2.6 million. Thus, Trump can get on stage (or heck, run a TV ad) and brag that an established right-leaning think tank believes his tax policy proposals will create twice as many jobs as his competitors'. I mean, it's not as if his establishment-backed rivals have much standing to criticize him over fiscal responsibility. And if the short-fingered GOP front-runner needs another conservative celebrity endorsement, he can just quote this tweet from Grover Norquist. What better sell are you going to get than "Jobs. Jobs. Jobs."?[11]

Keep in mind that Donald Trump, while proposing a budget that would lead to unprecedented deficit spending, simultaneously urged fellow Republicans to ignore the constitutional limits on their power and pursue hostage-taking tactics to unilaterally force the government to default on its debt *unless federal spending is cut.* On October 18, 2015, he told Fox News Sunday that he supports US debt default, saying that he would seek a "very big pound of flesh"[12] in cuts in exchange for raising the debt limit.

---

11. Jordan Weissmann, "A Conservative Group Analyzed Donald Trump's Tax Plan. The Results are Kind of Hilarious," MoneyBox, *Slate*, Sept. 29, 2015, http://www.slate.com/blogs/moneybox/2015/09/29/donald _trump_s_tax_plan_the_tax_foundation_says_it_would_add_at_least _10.html.

12. "Trump Flexes Fiscal Conservative Creds, But Wants to Stay

Fox News, a guilty party to this complete cognitive dissonance, not only does not call him out on the contradiction between his own plans to lavishly spend above means and a mania for others to cut spending, but rewards Trump with the headline "Trump Flexes Fiscal Conservative Creds."[13] The "very big pound of flesh," however, is no more than political opportunism masked as fiscal constraint. The statement that preceded his demand is revealing: "I want to be unpredictable." The principle of freedom is about constraints evenly applied to those who hold power. More than anything, Trump wants to reserve the right to do what Trump wants to do. And this message resonates well with the conservative primary base.

Beyond budget plans of the primary candidates and their near universal embrace of supply-side dogma, three additional factors augur poorly for fiscal responsibility from today's GOP. First, note that the estimates on incremental debt incurred by their budget proposals (for Trump the math would suggest $1.9 million per job created) assume a normalized spending pattern over the forecasted ten-year period. But the established pattern for conservatives in the executive office is to accelerate government spending significantly. Indeed, current Republican candidates almost across the board have already promised to greatly increase defense spending while not specifying spending cuts in clear detail.

Second, the conservative party has become more conservative, both in terms of how it is represented in Congress and the constituency that identifies itself as conservative. If a Republican

'Unpredictable' on Debt Ceiling, Other Key Issues," FoxNews.com, published Oct. 18, 2015, http://www.foxnews.com/politics/2015/10/18/trump-flexes-fiscal-conservative-creds-but-wants-to-stay-unpredictable-on-debt0.html.

13. Ibid.

were elected President in 2016 with control of both houses of Congress (as would likely be the case), the forces that would argue for restraint would be weaker than they have ever been before. The influential advisors who fought the supply-siders in the Reagan Administration, such as David Gergen, Richard Darman, James Baker, Ken Durberstein, and Howard Baker, are complete anathema to today's Republican Party. "When media reports use 'fiscal conservative,' they're usually referring to supply-siders. They call them fiscal conservatives because the old fiscal conservatism has disappeared from the conservative movement. Supply-side economics has become the fiscal policy of conservatives."[14] This observation was made by Chait in 2007; it is, if anything, more true today.

Third, overall federal spending disproportionately benefits conservative voting districts. David Frum described this facet of what he has termed the "crisis of followership" in the Republican Party:

> Republicans find it difficult to produce budget plans because we (or at least our leaders) do know how the federal government spends its money: on our voters. For all the angry talk-radio talk about Obama's "gimme-dat" coalition, the awkward fact is that it's the GOP that commands the support of America's top "takers": the older, the rural, the Southern. If you want to close the budget gap, you won't get very far by squeezing young black single mothers —not compared to what you'll find in the defense budget, or in Medicare, or in Social Security, or in the farm budget, etc. etc. etc. Junk facts like the Heritage Foundation's claim that we spend $1 trillion a year on "welfare" are intended to obscure this truth. (The biggest chunk of that $1 trillion is Medicaid spending, and the biggest and fastest-growing

---

14. Chait, *The Big Con*, 44.

program in Medicaid is nursing-home care.) It's not easy
for the party that represents the biggest beneficiaries of
government spending to formulate plans to reduce government spending.[15]

Note how Chait's analysis differs from Frum's. For Chait, a small
elite group of zealots is hoodwinking a large constituency that
cares about fiscal restraint. For Frum, the vexing problem that
Republicans face is closer to the reverse. Its leaders find it difficult to budget sensibly because the broad base of their constituency likes their disproportionate take of federal spending.

But the reality is more simple: fiscal restraint is simply not
a priority. The mistake that both Frum and Chait make is the
assumption that *somewhere* conservatives care more about fiscal restraint than about simply selectively cutting funding for
those specific programs they oppose morally and politically.
Understanding conservatism as a temperament appears to offer a much better explanation. As Hayek would state, "that the
conservative opposition to too much government control is not
a matter of principle but is concerned with the particular aims
of government is clearly shown in the economic sphere."[16]

The freedom-fraud narrative is powerful. In some ways the
freedom narrative is propagated with pure cynicism, but in most
respects American conservatives at least partly believe their
own misguided crusade, choosing the most selective interpre-
tation of facts to keep their fiscal fantasy coherent. It affects
the press as well, since it is difficult to know where to begin
speaking to today's conservatives without partly playing along

15. David Frum, "Wanna Beat Obama? Here's How," *Daily Beast*, Dec. 13,
2012, http://www.thedailybeast.com/articles/2012/12/13/the-alternative-
to-doomsday-conservatism.html.

16. Friedrich A. Hayek, *The Constitution of Liberty* (Chicago: University
of Chicago Press, 1960), 403.

with the narrative. A October 21, 2015 interview between political reporter Mike Grunwald and Grover Norquist provides a good example. The interview is a kind of polite affirmation of Norquist's worldview, though Grunwald often pushes back with basic facts that are devastating to it and, at the same time, so obvious that it would be journalistic malpractice to withhold them. Many of the exchanges follow this type of back and forth:

> GN: Government spending has decreased from 24 percent of GDP to 20 percent in just three years. Huge.

> MG: The last time Republicans controlled Washington, it, um, wasn't like this.

> GN: That was before the Tea Party. When people ask what happened to the Tea Party, part of the answer is it moved into Congress. The other answer is it fundamentally transformed the Republican Party. Republicans were already on board with step one: Don't raise any taxes. That's the pledge. They were mostly OK with step two: Cut taxes at every opportunity. What was missing, and it was painfully obvious under George W. Bush, was spending restraint. It wasn't on their list of things to do. Every crisis, from September 11 to the flooding in New Orleans to the crash, the answer was spend money. Never reform government. It was always: spend money. The Tea Party changed that. There were about a million people in the streets. And those rallies were before any significant tax increase passed under Obama. They were rallies against spending. Against bailouts. Against the stimulus.[17]

17. Michael Grunwald, "Grover Norquist Isn't Finished," The Agenda, *Politico*, Oct. 21, 2015, http://www.politico.com/agenda/story/2015/10/grover-norquist-tax-interview-000288.

What Norquist is claiming here is worth scrutiny. To be clear, Norquist has had a highly successful influence-peddling career. As the leader of Americans for Tax Reform, he is one of the most powerful conservative lobbyists in Washington. He presides over the Wednesday Group, a weekly meeting that has been called "the Grand Central Station of the conservative movement."[18] Most people might characterize him as a shrewd, hard-headed operator. But naïve zealotry, too, seems to fuel his endless drive, and that is evident in this interview.

The interesting question is, what has his influence wrought? His entire strategy of maniacally focusing on reducing tax rates has been most often associated with a corresponding lack of fiscal discipline and increased government spending. For the duration of his three-decade-plus career, he has acknowledged that government spending, which determines the size of the government, has not actually been the main conservative priority: "It was not on their list of things to do." That's some admission for a small-government crusader. Those were the people that he helped put into power. But never mind, he says, now finally—step three—now's the time spending cuts will work.

It does not to occur to him that there is a reason his career took off by asking politicians to take the pledge never to raise taxes (regardless of spending requirements or obligations), instead of a pledge never to increase spending. As pointed out by Kevin Williamson, cutting taxes is easy, but cutting spending is hard. A spending pledge would be dead on arrival for the simple reason that it does not offer an easy out. Peddling this easy out under the guise of liberty is what has propelled his influence.

It does not occur to him that the Tea Party protesters—the same individuals who make the case to "keep government out of their Medicare"[19]—may not be the white-knight force of fiscal restraint that finally comes to save his day. It does not occur to him that a good part of Donald Trump's appeal to that same Tea Party following is that he has promised *not* to touch Medicare and to *greatly* increase defense spending (all the while making historically large tax cuts).

It also does not occur to him that even as he professes to be stridently against Washington special interests, there is a simple racketeering logic to his anti-tax scheme: take money from the people who benefit the most from low taxes—the very wealthy and those enjoying tax loopholes—and funnel that money to politicians who agree to be in his policy straitjacket.

For Norquist, there is an odd naiveté reminiscent of Graham Green's *The Quiet American* of someone who thinks he is saving the world while standing in a pool of blood that he created. When the blood is drawn to his attention, he simply ignores it, not comprehending or else considering it incidental to the great, distant idealized objective: "My goal is to reduce the size of government by half over 25 years, and then to do that again in 25 years, and eventually get it small enough that if you wanted you could drown it in the tub. That's doable over time. It's a long-term goal," he says to Grunwald.[20]

The key to understanding the state of our nation's finances is not to be distracted or thrown off by such soaring rhetoric. Conservatives by temperament tend to care about matters other than political freedom, and only use the language of freedom to promote other priorities. The ascent of the most extreme version of supply-side economic theory is simply a more elaborate

19. Timothy Noah, "Why Tea Party Seniors Love Paul Ryan," *The New Republic*, August 15, 2012, https://newrepublic.com/article/106198/timothy-noah-why-tea-party-senior-citizens-love-paul-ryan

20. Grunwald, "Grover Norquist Isn't Finished."

construction of this tendency. The triumph of the extreme version of supply-side economic theory is a triumph over fiscal conservatism, not a triumph for fiscal conservatism; its enduring power is owed to the manner in which it greatly helps reconcile the conservative aversion to restraint with their nominal belief in liberty, where restraint is a central principle.

Why Conservatives Are So Quick to Abandon Liberty in the Face of Security Threats

In keeping with his penchant for bluster and showmanship, on December 7—Pearl Harbor Day—Donald Trump announced that in response to the San Bernardino attacks he would support the dramatic step of banning all Muslims from entering the country. The initial—perhaps hopeful—reporting suggested that his proposal "evoked outrage from across the political spectrum."[21] And it was true that Republican leaders from Paul Ryan and Lindsey Graham to even Dick Cheney spoke out against the proposal, some very forcefully.

But the Republican conservative base did not in fact express "outrage." To the contrary, a Bloomberg Politics and Purple Insights poll soon after the announcement indicated the proposal was supported by Republican Primary voters with 65% in favor, 22% opposed, and 13% who did not know.[22] Polls released

21. Reid J. Epstein and Peter Nicholas, "Donald Trump Calls for Ban on Muslim Entry into U.S.," *Wall Street Journal*, Dec. 7, 2015, http://www.wsj.com/articles/donald-trump-calls-for-ban-on-muslim-entry-into-u-s-1449526104.

22. John McCormick, "Bloomberg Politics Poll: Nearly Two Thirds of Likely GOP Primary Voters Back Trumps Muslim Ban," *Bloomberg*, Dec. 9, 2015, http://www.bloomberg.com/politics/articles/2015-12-09/bloomberg-politics-poll-trump-muslim-ban-proposal.

shortly after his Monday announcement showed continued enthusiasm for Trump's candidacy.[23] If anything, Trump's numbers had improved.

Understanding conservatism as a temperament rather than a political philosophy, as Hayek maintains, helps explain the response to the Trump proposal. That a conservative by temperament may be less inclined to oppose "arbitrary power so long as it is used for what he regards as the right purposes" helps us make sense of why such a large portion of the Republican base favored a proposal that so directly contradicts the US Constitution. In Hayek's view, the truer conservative response to a security threat is a desire for a leader who won't be squeamish, who won't be held up by technicalities, who will go ahead and take the steps that they see as obvious to make them safe.

A Frank Luntz focus group with 29 Trump supporters held on December 9, 2015, just following Trump's announcement, provides a revealing example. A reporter from the *Economist* who attended the focus-group session made several interesting observations. First, the conservatives in the group included much more than the stereotypical disaffected Trump supporter. Second, they were either supportive of Trump's Muslim ban or their support for Trump was unaffected by his proposal.

What they described was not so much primal rage as deep resentment that they, as individuals, have a sense of how

23. "CBS News/New York Times Poll, December 4-8, 2015," conducted by SSRS of Media, PA on behalf of CBS News and the New York Times, *CBS News*, Dec. 10, 2015, http://www.cbsnews.com/news/poll-donald-trump-top-ted-cruz-second-hillary-clinton-over-bernie-sanders/.; "WBUR Poll, New Hampshire 2016 Republican Primary, December 6-8, 2015," conducted by MassINC Polling Group on behalf of WBUR, *WBUR Boston's NPR News Station*, Dec. 11, 2015, http://www.wbur.org/2015/12/11/donald-trump-new-hampshire-support-climbs.

America should be, and of how it is going wrong. They are sure that they know exactly how dangerous many Muslims are, and how the country is made less safe by admitting them. They find it self-evident that this president is destroying the country. But sneering, elite political correctness smothers them and silences them and seeks to deny the evidence they are sure that they have seen with their own eyes and heard with their own ears.[24]

The really interesting feature of the focus group was their shared ire, directed not only at President Obama, but at the Republican establishment as well. In many respects, Trump supporters know who they are as conservatives and intuitively are calling out the freedom fraud when they hear it from Republican leaders (at least on this point). For example, consider the distance between how most Trump supporters respond to a proposed Muslim ban and a typical mainstream response, like the one reported in the *Washington Post* soon after the proposal was introduced, "Experts: Trump's Muslim Entry Ban Idea 'Ridiculous,' 'Unconstitutional'":

> "That's blatantly unconstitutional if it excludes U.S. citizens because they are Muslims. It's ridiculous," said Richard Friedman, a law professor at the University of Michigan. He cited the U.S. Constitution's equal protection clause and the First Amendment's doctrine of freedom of religion. Barring Muslims who are not U.S. citizens from entering the country may not violate U.S. law in the same way, the experts said, because the Constitution's protections generally do not apply to people outside the nation's borders.

24. Lexington, "Just a Regular Guy: Donald Trump's Supporters Reveal Why They Back Him," *Economist*, Dec. 11, 2015, http://www.economist.com/blogs/democracyinamerica/2015/12/just-regular-guy.

But that's irrelevant, they said, because Trump's plan
would break many principles of international law and
agreements the U.S. has signed with other nations. "We
have treaties, all sorts of relationships with other countries," said Palma Yanni, a D.C. immigration lawyer and
past president of the American Immigration Lawyers Association. "I'm sure it would violate innumerable treaties if
we suddenly started banning citizens of NATO countries,
of Southeast Asian countries." ... But the experts said that
Trump's proposal would go much further because it tar-
gets religion, not a nationality or region. "A nation could
argue that national security provides a rationale for bar-
ring immigrants from particular countries engaged in civil
wars," ... [said Jonathan Turley, a constitutional law expert
at George Washington University]. "But those rationales
fall by the wayside when you are using an arbitrary criteria
[sic] like religion."[25]

For the pure conservative, the above report reads like an op-ed,
and one that they would probably object to strongly. The concerns that pertain to maintaining a free society as articulated
by the constitutional experts above are explicitly not the concerns of the Trump supporters. To the contrary, those principles
—and, worse still, international treaties—are the rigid rules
that they find inane in the context of a perceived threat.

Trump's Muslim-ban proposal creates a twofold dilemma for
right-of-center conservative leaders: first, how to maintain the

25. Jerry Markon, "Experts: Trump's Muslim Entry Ban Idea 'Ridiculous,' 'Unconstitutional,'" *Washington Post*, Dec. 7, 2015, https://www.
washingtonpost.com/politics/experts-trumps-muslim-entry-ban-idea-
ridiculous-unconstitutional/2015/12/07/d44a970a-9d47-11e5-bce4-
708fe33e3288_story.html.

freedom fraud (how to equate freedom with conservatism) in the context of a proposal that appeals to conservative tendencies, and yet is so obviously at odds with the principles of religious tolerance and a free society? To the *Economist* reporter covering the focus-group session, the contradiction on display was strong enough for him to correctly note that speaking out against the proposal carries large risks for Republican leadership.

> When Republican leaders in Congress and presidential rivals this week denounced [Trump's] call to ban Muslim travelers as "unconservative" and an affront to American values, that may have been a high-risk tactic. For his supporters want to be told that they are right, and good people. They are sick of being chided, and put down and corrected—even when they are citing "evidence" that is half- or wholly-nonsense.[26]

It is quite fitting here that the reporter places the description of the Muslim ban proposal as "unconservative" in quotation marks. What the reporter intuitively understands is that Trump's proposal is indeed conservative, not liberal, in the sense that it appeals to conservative temperament. The second dilemma faced by conservative leaders is if they don't speak out forcefully against the Muslim ban, they risk losing support outside of the conservative base. As noted by author and former Reagan official Bruce Bartlett just after Trump's proposal, "[c]riticism of Trump on the Right exists but mainly because fear he will lose and bring down GOP, not because his views are beyond the pale."[27]

---

26. Lexington, "Just a Regular Guy."

27. Bruce Bartlett, Twitter post, Dec. 11, 2015, https://twitter.com/BruceBartlett/status/675408399576756226.

So when House Majority Leader Paul Ryan responded to Trump's proposal by saying "What was proposed yesterday: This is not conservatism ... This is not what our party stands for and, more importantly, it's not what our country stands for," the conservative base is not exactly buying it. They smell insincere rhetoric, and insofar as conservatism is concerned, they are largely correct.

"Restrain This White House": George W. Bush and Security

Of course, the quick rebuke on the part of conservative leaders to Trump's proposal was welcome. It certainly limited near-term reputational damage to the United States with allies and the international community. But unfortunately, there is not a sharp distinction between Trump's response to terrorism, how conservatives in recent history have responded to terrorism, or even how Trump's leading primary competitors proposed addressing terrorist threats themselves. The common denominator is often a rejection of the "politically correct" restraints that prevent our leaders from taking what they see as the obvious actions that would make us safe. The biggest difference is that Trump is more direct. He does not conflate conservatism with a political philosophy of freedom or our founding principles—he dispenses with the freedom-fraud rhetoric almost entirely.

Starting with George W. Bush, there's more continuity than difference in how conservatives have responded to security threats. One way to view right-of-center politics prior to the second Bush is as an uneasy alliance between classic liberals and conservatives by temperament. In the face of the threat from the Soviet Union and communism, this alliance had a common purpose. Some of these classic liberals may have considered themselves to be conservative, but they really played a crucial role in *checking* conservative tendencies on the Right. As the menace of communism faded, so did the bonds of the alliance.

Perhaps the defining characteristic of the Bush II Presidency in the sphere of national security and international affairs was a consistent and methodical effort to eliminate constraints on executive power. The classic liberals who had held power on the Right in previous years and stood for principles of restraint were mostly overrun. Right-of-center, conservative temperament became mostly unchecked.

The most poignant and clear rendering of events at that time comes from those on the Right who took classic liberal principles seriously, but who inappropriately aligned themselves with conservatives. One such individual is Bruce Fein, a former Associate Deputy Attorney General under Reagan. To be sure, Fein has advocated against what he considered to be executive overreach under President Clinton and, more recently, under President Obama.

But Fein's view was that George W. Bush's "super-imperial" presidency marked a unique break from the past in its disdain for the rule of law and its virtually unfettered and indefinite claims to executive power. In his view, George W. Bush "staked out powers that are a universe beyond any other administration."[28] It is easy to forget the scope with which executive power was rapidly consolidated in the face of security threats after the September 11 attacks. A 2006 short essay by Fein in *Washington Monthly*, "Restrain This White House," is a worthwhile reminder. Bush led, and Republicans in Congress followed, including most, if not all, of the Republicans who have more recently strenuously objected to Trump's Muslim-ban proposal.

---

28. Mayer, "The Hidden Power."

Republicans in Congress have bowed to the president's scorn for the rule of law and craving for secret government. They have voted against Democratic Sen. Russell Feingold's resolution to rebuke Bush for violating federal statutes and crippling checks and balances. They have resisted brandishing either the power of the purse or the contempt power (with which it can compel testimony) to end the president's violation of FISA and to force full disclosure of his secret foreign-intelligence programs. Indeed, the Republican chairman of the Senate Judiciary Committee, Arlen Specter, is sponsoring a bill that in substance endorses President Bush's FISA illegalities and authorizes an electronic-surveillance program warrant that would enable the NSA to spy on Americans indiscriminately without the particularized suspicion of wrongdoing required by the Fourth Amendment. ... The most frightening claim made by Bush with congressional acquiescence is reminiscent of the *lettres de cachet* of prerevolutionary France. (Such letters, with which the king could order the arrest and imprisonment of subjects without trial, helped trigger the storming of the Bastille.) In the aftermath of 9/11, Mr. Bush maintained that he could pluck any American citizen out of his home or off of the sidewalk and detain him indefinitely on the president's finding that he was an illegal combatant. No court could second-guess the president. Bush soon employed such monarchial power to detain a few citizens and to frighten would-be dissenters, and Republicans in Congress either cheered or fiddled like Nero while the Constitution burned.[29]

It is in fact hard to overstate the lengths to which George W. Bush went to remove constraints on his power in the context of

29. Fein, "Restrain This White House."

security threats, and it is worthwhile to recount the observations of historians and constitutional experts at the time. These two observations, noted by reporter Jane Mayer in a *New Yorker* piece on Dick Cheney's Chief Counsel David Addington, were not atypical:

> Scott Horton, a professor at Columbia Law School, and the head of the New York Bar Association's International Law committee, said that Addington and a small group of Administration lawyers who share his views had attempted to "overturn two centuries of jurisprudence defining the limits of the executive branch. They've made war a matter of dictatorial power." The historian Arthur Schlesinger, Jr., who defined Nixon as the extreme example of Presidential overreaching in his book *The Imperial Presidency* (1973), said he believes that Bush "is more grandiose than Nixon."[30]

A more detailed and fascinating portrait of the Bush presidency and the actors who played a central role in the unprecedented expansion of executive power is provided by Jack Goldsmith, a conservative academic who advanced quickly in government after departing the University of Chicago to become a top lawyer in the Department of Defense and then led the Justice Department's Office of Legal Counsel (OLC) for nine months from October of 2003 to June of 2004. Per Goldsmith's account, he was chosen to replace Jay Bybee as the head of the OLC in 2003 only after Attorney General John Ashcroft rejected Bush II's first choice, Deputy Assistant US Attorney General in the Office of Legal Counsel John Yoo.

Once in the job, Goldsmith quickly gained a new appreciation of Addington's and Yoo's conservatism. What he found was an extreme aversion to any type of constraint on executive

---

30. Mayer, "The Hidden Power."

power. In the aftermath of the September 11 attacks, Yoo was the primary author of memos that defined the president's authority during the newly declared "war on terror." These memos were written from the Attorney General's Office of Legal Counsel where responsibility for such important matters resides. We don't know all of the legal opinions rendered by Yoo's prolific pen in the two years that followed the September 11 attacks. However, his notorious "torture memos" provide a good example of the essentially limitless power that he granted to the presidency. These powers were accorded for a vaguely defined, potentially indefinite "war on terror." Even as a very conservative lawyer, Goldsmith describes the first August 1, 2002 OLC memo like this:

> The opinion identified torture with acts that cause the amount of pain "associated with a sufficiently serious physical condition or injury such as death, organ failure, or serious impairment of body functions." Any action that fell short of these extreme conditions could not, in OLC's view, be torture. Even if the interrogators crossed this hard-to-reach line and committed torture, OLC opined, they could still avoid criminal liability by invoking a necessity defense (on the theory that torture may be necessary to prevent a catastrophic harm) or self-defense (on the theory that the interrogators were acting to save the country and themselves). Finally, OLC concluded, the torture law violated the President's constitutional commander-in-chief powers, and thus did not bind executive branch officials, because it prevented the President "from gaining the intelligence he believes necessary to prevent attacks upon the United States." The message of the August 1, 2002, OLC opinion was indeed clear: violent acts aren't necessarily torture; if you do torture, you probably have a defense; and even if

you don't have a defense, the torture law doesn't apply if you act under color of presidential authority. CIA interrogators and their supervisors, under pressure to get information about the next attack, viewed the opinion as a "golden shield," as one CIA official later called it, that provided enormous comfort."[31]

What puzzled Goldsmith about these memos was their gratuitously limitless vision of presidential power and their lack of precedent, legal or otherwise.

OLC might have limited its set-aside of the torture statute to the rare situations in which the President believed that exceeding the law was necessary in an emergency, leaving the torture law intact in the vast majority of instances. But the opinion went much further. "Any effort by Congress to regulate the interrogation of battlefield detainees would violate the Constitution's sole vesting of the Commander-in-Chief authority in the President," the August 2002 memo concluded. This extreme conclusion has no foundation in prior OLC opinions, or in judicial decisions, or in any other source of law. And the conclusion's significance sweeps far beyond the interrogation opinion or the torture statute. It implies that many other federal laws that limit interrogation—anti-assault laws, the 1996 War Crimes Act, and the Uniform Code of Military Justice—are also unconstitutional, a conclusion that would have surprised the many prior presidents who signed or ratified those laws, or complied with them during wartime.[32]

31. Jack Goldsmith, *The Terror Presidency: Law and Judgment Inside the Bush Administration* (New York: W. W. Norton & Company, 2007), 171-72.

32. Ibid., 177.

It is also important not to be thrown off by the fact that Yoo's memos said several different things. On the one hand, he took care to define torture in a very narrow, extreme way. In this way, the opinion opened the door for "rough treatment" that then would not be regarded as torture legally. He also offered opinions on the legality of specific "enhanced interrogation" techniques such as waterboarding, arguing that those techniques did not meet the legal definition of torture. At the same time, he went on to state that whatever an individual did was okay as long as he or she were acting under the color of presidential authority. Yoo's own view on his memos makes this very clear. In a 2004 debate with Douglas Cassel, a Notre Dame legal scholar, he said the following:

> Cassel: If the president deems that he's got to torture somebody, including by crushing the testicles of the person's child, there is no law that can stop him?
>
> Yoo: No treaty.
>
> Cassel: Also, no law by Congress—that is what you wrote in the August 2002 memo ...
>
> Yoo: I think it depends on why the president thinks he needs to do that.[33]

It is important to reiterate that Yoo was not a rogue actor in the George W. Bush administration. As already noted, according to Goldsmith, he was Bush II's first choice in 2003 to replace

---

33. "John Yoo on Torture," YouTube video, 1:06, posted by "crooksandliars," Nov. 25, 2008, https://www.youtube.com/watch?v=bO2p0KHyzpw.

Jay Bybee as director of the Office of Legal Counsel, the crucial office in the Department of Justice that clarifies and defines presidential authority. Per Goldsmith's account, many of the decisions on defining this authority were driven by Vice President Dick Cheney and in particular his long-time legal advisor, David Addington. Moreover, one of the most interesting and revealing aspects of Goldsmith's account is of the personalities of those in this small but highly influential circle of Bush II advisors. In particular, the description of Addington very much dovetails with a temperament averse to restraint.

> Addington once expressed his general attitude toward accommodation when he said, "We're going to push and push and push until some larger force makes us stop." He and, I presumed, his boss viewed power as the absence of constraint. These men believed that the President would be best equipped to identify and defeat the uncertain, shifting, and lethal new enemy by eliminating all hurdles to the exercise of his power. They had no sense of trading constraint for power. It seemed never to occur to them that it might be possible to increase the President's strength and effectiveness by accepting small limits on his prerogatives in order to secure more significant support from Congress, the courts, or allies.[34]

It is worth noting here the importance of defining conservatism properly and of understanding how conservatism tends against legal constraint. In many ways, Addington's approach to governance is nearly diametrically opposed to that of right-of-center classic liberals like Bruce Fein. But Fein, like other

---

34. Goldsmith, *The Terror Presidency*, 149-50.

classic liberals, mislead themselves and do a tremendous dis-
service by defining themselves as conservative, and equating
conservatism with freedom, as he did at the start of the short
piece I quoted from *Washington Monthly*: "The most conservative
principle of the Founding Fathers was distrust of unchecked
power."[35]

To the contrary, conservatives tend to distrust the mecha-
nisms that do check power. Without question, the principle to
which Fein refers to is a liberal principle, or at least it tends to
run counter to conservative temperament. Consider Thomas
Jefferson's famous quote: "In questions of power, then, let no
more be heard of confidence in man, but bind him down from
mischief by the chains of the Constitution."[36] How starkly different is that opinion from Addington's approach to seek as
much latitude for presidential authority as possible and "to
push and push and push until some larger force makes us stop";
or from Yoo's response to Cassel on the justification for torture:
"I think it depends on why the president thinks he needs to
do that."

Much has been written about the consequences of the
ideas that Bush II, Cheney, Addington, Yoo, and others put into
action with regard to presidential power, torture, and fighting
the "war on terror." The key point here is to make abundantly
clear which direction conservatism tends, and how conservative tendencies move in opposition to the constraints that are
intrinsic to the political philosophy of a free society.

---

35. Fein, "Restrain This White House."

36. Thomas Jefferson, "Draft of Kentucky Resolution 1789," quoted in
E. D. Warfield, *The Kentucky Resolutions of 1798* (New York, 1894), 157-58,
quoted in Friedrich A. Hayek, *The Constitution of Liberty* (Chicago:
University of Chicago Press, 1960), 246.

The Contempt for Treaties and International Law

The aversion that conservatives have to the even application of laws and constraints that apply domestically is, if anything, greatly magnified in international affairs. Here the attitude toward international treaties or laws that restrain the action of the United States as a country lies somewhere between high suspicion and utter contempt.

A useful example is the contrast between Bush senior and Bush II in international affairs. When Saddam Hussein invaded Kuwait in August of 1990, the immediate response from the first Bush administration was a far-reaching and intense diplomatic effort. The ratcheting of diplomatic pressure was exercised through the UN Security Council, culminating in the January 15, 1991 deadline in UN Security Council Resolution 678, which authorized all member states "to use all means necessary" to get Saddam Hussein and his forces out of Kuwait and bring him into compliance with previous Security Council Resolutions.

When George H. W. Bush prosecuted the war with a coalition of allies, he quickly ousted Saddam's forces from Kuwait and then, much to the intense dismay of the conservative wing within his cabinet, chose not to pursue Saddam's forces into Baghdad and occupy Iraq. There were, of course, very good practical reasons not to occupy Iraq. But the other major factor for Bush senior was very much a matter of international law and precedent. The international process had authorized the defense and restoration of the borders of Kuwait, not the invasion and occupation of Iraq. And, in international law, there is a significant difference between a defensive war and a war of aggression. Supreme Court Justice and lead prosecutor at the Nuremberg trials Robert H. Jackson defined the difference at Nuremberg:

War inevitably is a course of killings, assaults, deprivations of liberty, and destruction of property. An honestly defensive war is, of course, legal and saves those lawfully conducting it from criminality. But inherently criminal acts cannot be defended by showing that those who committed them were engaged in a war, when war itself is illegal. The very minimum legal consequence of the treaties making aggressive wars illegal is to strip those who incite or wage them of every defense the law ever gave, and to leave war-makers subject to judgment by the usually accepted principles of the law.

In this way,

To initiate a war of aggression, therefore, is not only an international crime; it is *the supreme international crime*, differing only from other war crimes in that it contains within itself the accumulated evil of the whole.[37]

The overarching effort of the Nuremberg trials was not only to bring Nazi criminals to justice, but to set the precedent so that "the record on which we judge these defendants today is the record on which history will judge us tomorrow" and to make international law "unequivocal in classifying armed aggression as an international crime instead of a national right."[38]

Bush senior fought in World War II as an aviator, and he himself was a diplomat as the Ambassador to the United Nations.

---

37. Benjamin B. Ferencz, "Enabling the International Criminal Court to Punish Aggression," *Washington University Global Studies Law Review* 6, no. 3 (2007): 552, http://openscholarship.wustl.edu/cgi/viewcontent.cgi?article=1149&context=law_globalstudies.

38. Ibid., 553.

These experiences prior to becoming the nation's 41st President may have informed his response to Saddam Hussein's aggression and influenced his decision not to invade Baghdad and control Iraq, much to the chagrin of the conservative wing in his cabinet. In *A World Transformed*, a 1998 book that he co-authored with his national security advisor, Brent Scowcroft, Bush senior stated that "we had been self-consciously trying to set a pattern for handling aggression in the post-Cold War world. Going in and occupying Iraq, thus unilaterally exceeding the U.N.'s mandate, would have destroyed the precedent of international response to aggression we hoped to establish."[39]

In addition, during the 1990s, Bush senior spoke "out clearly for the rule of law and supported the idea of an International Criminal Court (ICC)"[40] to deter wars of aggression. The establishment of the ICC would have been the institutional realization of what Robert S. Jackson, the United States, and our World War II allies had begun at Nuremberg nearly fifty years before. This longstanding goal was within reach when delegates from 120 countries agreed to terms for the ICC, voting in favor of the Rome Statute in 1998. The treaty, however, was never ratified by the United States.

On his last day in office, President Bill Clinton signed the treaty as a symbolic gesture to show the United States intended to eventually ratify the treaty if certain modifications were made. However, he did not submit the treaty for ratification by Congress as he knew he did not have the two-thirds consent of

---

39. George Bush and Brent Scowcroft, *A World Transformed: The Collapse of the Soviet Empire, the Unification of Germany, Tiananmen Square, the Gulf War* (New York: Alfred A. Knopf, 1998), Chapter 19.

40. Benjamin B. Ferencz, "Tribute to Nuremberg Prosecutor Jackson," *Pace International Law Review* 16, no. 2 (2004): 373, http://digitalcommons. pace.edu/cgi/viewcontent.cgi?article=1168&context=pilr.

the US Senate required by the Constitution. Senator Jesse Helms of North Carolina, who was Chairman of the Foreign Relations Committee, staunchly opposed any foreign court ever having jurisdiction over any Americans, a view shared widely in conservative circles.

The concern for adherence to the procedures within the UN Security Council and international precedent within the Bush senior administration could not contrast more starkly with the administration of his son. When Bush II came to power, his foreign policy and defense team comprised many of the conservatives who had wanted the US to invade Baghdad and occupy Iraq in 1991. They included Paul Wolfowitz, Deputy Secretary of Defense; Douglas Feith, Under Secretary of Defense for Policy; Lewis "Scooter" Libby, the vice president's Chief of Staff; Elliott Abrams, the National Security Council staffer for Near East, Southwest Asian, and North African Affairs; Richard Perle, a member of the Defense Policy Board; and John Bolton, Under Secretary of State for Arms Control and International Security.

To be sure, the Bush II cabinet included individuals who were not part of the group that had favored occupying Iraq, such as Secretary of State Colin Powell. In addition, as surprising as it may seem now, Bush II ran for office on a platform of a humble foreign policy. "If we're an arrogant nation, they'll resent us; if we're a humble nation, but strong, they'll welcome us. And our nation stands alone right now in the world in terms of power, and that's why we've got to be humble, and yet project strength in a way that promotes freedom," he said in an October 12 debate with Al Gore.[41]

Almost immediately, the actual direction taken by Bush II

41. George W. Bush and Al Gore, "Presidential Debate," moderated by Jim Lehrer and excerpted by Ray Suarez, *PBS News Hour*, Oct. 12, 2000, http://www.pbs.org/newshour/bb/politics-july-dec00-for-policy_10-12/.

in foreign affairs contrasted sharply with that of his father and his pre-campaign rhetoric. By June of 2001, the direction was clear enough for conservative columnist Charles Krauthammer to triumphantly announce a new era, guided by "The Bush Doctrine." "Rather than contain American power within a vast web of constraining international agreements," he wrote, "the new unilateralism seeks to enhance American power and unashamedly deploy it on behalf of *self-defined* global ends."[42] In the column, Krauthammer lauded the Bush II administration's departure from the 1972 Anti-Ballistic Missile Treaty and Bush II's out-of-hand rejection of the Kyoto protocol on global warming, a "flamboyant demonstration of the new unilateralism."

Not mentioned in the column was the fact that upon entering office, the second Bush administration began immediately working to derail the International Criminal Court (ICC) and the US participation in it. As Under Secretary of State for Arms Control and International Security, John Bolton worked assiduously toward this end. When the US did formally pull out of the ICC in May of 2002, John Bolton declared it to be the "happiest moment" of his career in government.[43]

Following the September 11 attacks, the shift to a new unilateralism that had been hailed by Krauthammer was more formally codified in the "National Security Strategy of the United States," published on September 17, 2002.[44] This document

42. Charles Krauthammer, "The Bush Doctrine: 'New Unilateralism,'" *Houston Chronicle*, June 8, 2001, http://www.chron.com/opinion/editorials/article/Krauthammer-The-Bush-doctrine-new-2055304.php.

43. "Let the Child Live," International Criminal Court, *Economist*, Jan. 25, 2007, http://www.economist.com/node/8599155.

44. "The National Security Strategy of the United States of America, September 2002" Washington, DC, http://www.state.gov/documents/organization/63562.pdf.

emphasized the importance of unilateral, pre-emptive military action and contrasted sharply with the Bush I/Scowcroft vision of the post-Cold War world. The logic of this shift, and in some ways an important precursor to the US invasion of Iraq in 2003, was articulated in June of 2002 in "Power and Weakness," an essay by neoconservative Robert Kagan.

This essay was widely read and very influential within the senior ranks of the Bush II administration. The paper offers a grandiose, ideologically driven vision against international law and in particular on any restraints as applied to the United States, as it had now become the dominant worldwide military power. Such restraints were the province of weak countries. One fascinating facet of the paper was the suggestion that the Bush II administration from the start was leery of any international cooperation for the very reason that it would then provide a basis to tie the administration down in international law. For the Bush II administration, it was as if international laws and restraints themselves were as great a threat to the United States as that posed by Al Qaeda or other international foes. Kagan's essay provided a rationale for the US to forge ahead with preemptive military action where it saw fit in a way that need not bother with Europe's "Lilliputian threads" at all.

> Even after September 11th, when the Europeans offered their very limited military capabilities in the fight in Afghanistan, the United States resisted, fearing that European cooperation was a ruse to tie America down. The Bush administration viewed NATO's historic decision to aid the United States under Article V less as a boon than as a booby trap. ... Americans are powerful enough that they need not fear Europeans, even when bearing gifts. Rather than viewing the United States as a Gulliver tied down by Lilliputian

threads, American leaders should realize that they are hardly constrained at all, that Europe is not really capable of constraining the United States.[45]

With revealing language, Jack Goldsmith noted that Kagan's influential essay "gave structure to the intuitions that top administrative officials already possessed."[46] Those intuitions are the parts of conservative temperament that tend against constraints on power and the rule of law, most emphatically in international affairs. Neoconservative intellectuals like Kagan would probably strenuously object to being categorized as conservative in such a blunt way. At the same time, for all the historical and intellectual sweep of American neoconservatism, the common denominator between neoconservatives and conservatives such as Jesse Helms seems to be a simple, strong aversion to legal constraints on power, domestic or international. For the conservative by temperament, the battle against legal constraint is almost an end in and of itself.

* * *

From this vantage point, one can better understand the Republican presidential primary season in 2015–2016. We find the exact same suspicion/contempt of international law and international treaties. But during the Bush II years, the battle against international legal constraint was fought by senior members of his administration in a less visible way and/or was clothed in intellectual pretension. Now this contempt is not only openly

45. Robert Kagan, "Power and Weakness," *Policy Review* (June and July, 2002): 3.

46. Goldsmith, *The Terror Presidency*, 197.

acknowledged, but, in a kind of arms race against the very idea of inalienable rights, Republican candidates compete to be least constrained by international law in a direct appeal to conservatism unbound.

This process may have been kicked off by Ben Carson in February of 2015.

"Our military needs to know that they're not gonna be prosecuted when they come back, because somebody has said, 'You did something that was politically incorrect,'" the likely Republican candidate told his national television audience. "There is no such thing as a politically correct war. We need to grow up, we need to mature. If you're gonna have rules for war, you should just have a rule that says no war. Other than that, we have to win. Our life depends on it."[47]

One must wonder what Senator John McCain, decorated war veteran, former prisoner of war, and strong supporter of the Geneva Conventions, must think of Ben Carson, who, having never experienced war himself, is implicitly telling Senator McCain that he needs "to mature" and "to grow up."

When Carson initially made the statement in February of 2015, it was correctly reported as "A Rare Endorsement of War Crimes." By the end of 2015, this type of statement was no longer rare, by Carson or by others in the Republican primary field. Trump has echoed Carson's sentiments by saying that to

47. Steve Benen, "Carson Makes a Rare Endorsement of War Crimes," MaddowBlog, *MSNBC*, Feb. 17, 2015, http://www.msnbc.com/rachel-maddow-show/carson-makes-rare-endorsement-war-crimes.

defeat ISIS you can't fight a "politically correct" war and "you have to take out their families."[48] The purposeful murder of civilians during wartime is widely considered a crime against humanity. Specifically, under the US-signed Hague Conventions, the US has agreed not to intentionally use violence against civilian noncombatants during wartime.

Moreover, it is not as if Trump and Carson were simply oblivious to this point. To the contrary, the deliberate defiance of international law seemed to be an important signal that they intended to communicate to their base that they would be "tough" on terrorism and would not be bogged down by the rules that hampered those who were not "serious" about the problem of terrorism. Perhaps as a way of trying to keep pace with Carson and Trump, Ted Cruz promised to carpet-bomb areas controlled by ISIS until we find out if "sand can glow in the dark."[49] And Marco Rubio promised to greatly expand the number of prisoners in Guantanamo.[50] It is this type of competition to appeal to the conservative temperament that serves to undermine liberal principles. In chapter 2, we examine a similar type of competition with respect to religion and moral convictions.

48. Emily Atkin, "To Defeat ISIS, Trump Openly Suggests Committing War Crimes," *Think Progress*, http://thinkprogress.org/world/2015/12/03/3727303/donald-trump-kill-isis-family-members/.

49. Louis Jacobson, "Ted Cruz Misfires on Definition of 'Carpet Bombing' in GOP Debate," *Politifact*, Dec. 16, 2015, http://www.politifact.com/truth-o-meter/statements/2015/dec/16/ted-cruz/ted-cruz-misfires-definition-carpet-bombing-gop-de/.

50. Carol Rosenberg, "Rubio: I'd Grow Guantánamo," *Miami Herald*, April 13, 2015, http://www.miamiherald.com/news/nation-world/world/americas/guantanamo/article18449078.html.

Addendum to Chapter 1:
A Refresher on Restraint and Political Freedom

A fundamental principle of political liberty is limiting arbitrary power. We are free as individuals to the extent that we are not subject to arbitrary authority. We limit arbitrary authority by constraining ourselves and those who wield political power. The basic architecture of our Constitution is to divide governing functions and to set restraints on the various branches of government so as to avoid arbitrary power consolidated in a monarchy. The Bill of Rights goes a step further in ensuring the rights of minorities against the tyranny of the majority—democracy itself must be restrained to protect liberty.[51]

Beyond the Constitution and the Bill of Rights, the close connection between evenly applied restraints and freedom is embedded in our culture. When students graduate from Harvard Law School, they are handed diplomas that remind them to think of laws as the "wise restraints that make men free." Our national hymn "America the Beautiful" declares "America, America / God mend thine every flaw. / Confirm thy soul in self control/ Thy liberty in law."[52] In his famous speech, "The Spirit of Liberty," Judge Learned Hand rhetorically asked "And what is this liberty which must lie in the hearts of men and women? It is not the ruthless, the unbridled will; it is not freedom to do as one likes. That is the denial of liberty, and leads straight to its overthrow."[53]

51. An excellent contemporary account of this specific tension is explored by Fareed Zakaria in his book *The Future of Freedom, Illiberal Democracy at Home and Abroad* (New York: W. W. Norton & Company, 2003)

52. Zakaria, *The Future of Freedom, Illiberal Democracy at Home and Abroad*, 26.

53. Learned Hand, "The Spirit of Liberty" (speech delivered at "I Am an American Day," New York, NY, 1944), edited by Erik Bruun and Jay Crosby, http://www.providenceforum.org/spiritoflibertyspeech.

Chapter 2

Strong Moral Convictions
That Trump Political Principles

*When I say that the conservative lacks principles, I do not
mean to suggest that he lacks moral conviction. The typical
conservative is indeed usually a man of very strong moral
convictions. What I mean is that he has no political
principles which enable him to work with people whose
moral values differ from his own for a political order in
which both can obey their convictions. —F. A. Hayek*

In the last chapter, we took a close look at two areas—federal
spending and the response to security threats—where principles of restraint required for a free society clash with conservative tendencies to seek the exercise of power without restraint. In these two areas we saw that, directionally, conservative temperament moves toward unlimited government, not
limited government. To be clear, policy ideas that are consistent with the principles of a free society may very well start out
on the political right, but they are often overwhelmed by the
underlying temperament of conservatism. For example, the
modest version of supply-side economic theory has a logic and
is persuasive under very specific conditions, but as supply-side
theory has been fully embraced on the Right, it has been transformed into an all-purpose justification to avoid fiscal responsibility and reward favored constituencies. The continued misplaced association of supply-side theory with the idea of fiscal
restraint makes it all the more dangerous.

A similar pattern has taken place on the Right with respect
to morals and religious beliefs. By 2006, some libertarians and

classic liberals on the Right could bemoan the fact that what they had understood as conservatism had come to represent very much the opposite. Brink Lindsey wrote in CATO Commentary:

> The old formulation defined conservatism as the desire to protect traditional values *from* the intrusion of big government; the new one seeks to promote traditional values *through* the intrusion of big government. Just look at the causes that have been generating the real energy in the conservative movement of late: building walls to keep out immigrants, amending the Constitution to keep gays from marrying, and imposing sectarian beliefs on medical researchers and families struggling with end-of-life decisions.[1]

It is important to understand that the "old formulation" was not conservatism, but a classically liberal idea to which conservatives, and in particular religious conservatives, became temporarily allied. This alliance between religious conservatives and classic liberals had an obvious logic in the face of a threat from communism. Communism was a kind of secular fundamentalism that promised to completely uproot and destroy religion as well as private property and the other institutions of the "bourgeois" economy. The bond between religious conservatives and classic liberals was therefore a sensible defensive alliance against "developments which threaten their ideals equally,"[2] as suggested by Hayek.

But as the threat of communism has faded, the alliance lacks a justification, and those on the Right with sincere convictions

---

1. Brink Lindsey, "Liberaltarians," Commentary, *CATO Institute*, http://www.cato.org/publications/commentary/liberaltarians.

2. Hayek, *The Constitution of Liberty*, 397.

about the principles of a free society are oddly situated and poorly matched against conservatives. Conservative temperament tends to trump what is mislabeled as conservative political philosophy (classic liberalism). Hayek's insight that conservatives lack political principles that enable them to work with people whose moral values differ from their own for a political order in which both can obey their convictions again explains features of the American Right that would otherwise be hard to understand.

This chapter is divided into three sections. The first part examines what one might call the "freeligious conservative": the odd concoction of religious conservatism/fundamentalism, on the one hand, and the rhetoric of a free society, on the other. Here again we find that conservatism tends against religious toleration and the separation of church and state, which are bedrock principles of a free society. Second, we look more in depth at the temperament of certainty that is often associated with conservatism, fundamentalism, and authoritarianism. Understanding today's American Right as a "coalition of the certain" explains alliances that otherwise seem contradictory (for example, why is the the thrice-married, materialistic Donald Trump endorsed and strongly supported by the Christian evangelical Jerry Falwell?). Finally, understanding the "coalition of the certain" and the increased conservatism of the American Right helps explain the Right's strong and growing animus against compromise and associated dysfunction of the American Congress.

The "Freeligious" Conservative

Much has been written on the growing influence of the religious Right in American politics. Less discussed is that the growth of religious conservatism in politics seems to have taken place along with increasingly strident rhetoric on the Right about its unique role in defending a free society.

Straddling religious conservatism and the philosophy of a free society is an increasingly awkward and uncomfortable dance for right-of-center politicians. This awkwardness becomes especially visible when it comes to issues such as the separation of church and state. For example, when Paul Ryan responded to Trump's Muslim-ban proposal ("This is not conservatism ... This is not what our party stands for and, more importantly, it's not what our country stands for") he is wearing his "separation of church and state/religious freedom" hat, and equating conservatism with the philosophy of a free society. But he also needs to appeal to religious conservatives. He does this with opposing statements, albeit somewhat more ambiguous ones, like the one he made in the 2012 Vice Presidential debate ("I don't see how a person can separate their public life from their private life or from their faith").[3] For Hayek, "the spiritual and the temporal are different spheres that ought not to be confused."[4] In the debate, Ryan burnishes his conservative credentials by implying just the opposite. It is a very different hat, one that comports more closely with conservative temperament, and with religious fundamentalism. The odd fusing of these two hats yields what one might term the "freeligious" conservative.

Conservative leaders often deny there is a tension at all. However, the tension showed through quite clearly, particularly in the early stages of the Republican presidential primary races. In his 2012 campaign, conservative stalwart Rick Santorum was introduced by Reverend Dennis Terry, who believes that

---

3. Paul Ryan, "Transcript and Audio: Vice Presidential Debate," *NPR*, Oct. 11, 2012, http://www.npr.org/2012/10/11/162754053/transcript-biden-ryan-vice-presidential-debate.

4. Hayek, *The Constitution of Liberty*, 407.

the one rightful God to worship in America is Christian, and that whoever disagrees should simply "get out."

> I don't care what the naysayers say. This nation was founded as a Christian nation. The god of Abraham and the God of Isaac and the God of Jacob. There is only one God. There is only one God, and his name is Jesus. I'm tired of people telling me that I can't say those words. I'm tired of people telling us as Christians that we can't voice our beliefs or we can't [sic] no longer pray in public. Listen to me. If you don't love America, and you don't like the way we do things, I've got one thing to say, get out!... We don't worship Buddha, we don't worship Mohammed, we don't worship Allah. We worship God. We worship God's son Jesus Christ.[5]

After repeated questioning by reporters, Santorum disavowed this comment, but throughout 2012 the conservative base was clearly comfortable with Santorum's desire to put Christian values in the front and center of his political campaign.

As the Republican Party has become more conservative, it is not surprising to see religion and morals as central themes of the 2015–2016 Republican primary campaigns. It is telling that John Kasich, rightly considered by many as one of the more moderate Republican candidates, felt compelled to propose a new federal agency to promote Judeo-Christian values. Worse, he did this in the immediate aftermath of the November 13 attacks in Paris that killed 130 people. The implication was that

---

5. Arlette Saenz, "Rick Santorum Disagrees with Pastor's Statement about Non-Christians," *ABC News*, March 19, 2012, http://abcnews.go. com/blogs/politics/2012/03/rick-santorum-doesnt-agree-with-louisiana-pastors-statement-about-non-christians-in-america/.

the root cause of the attacks was a lack of Judeo-Christian values rather than the perversion of Islam by extremists.

Moreover, as noted by the nonprofit Americans United for Separation of Church and State, the melding of religion and politics is certainly not symmetrical between the American Left and the American Right. Indeed, the difference between the 2015–2016 Democratic primary race and the Republican primary race in this respect is stark:

> While things have been relatively quiet on the Democratic side when it comes to the intersection of religion and politics, the same can't be said for the Republicans. The GOP race has been infused with religion from the start as a crowded field of candidates competes to win the support of the Religious Right. These voters make up a large percentage of the party's base, and they tend to turn out for primaries. Social conservatives have a plethora of candidates to choose from. Former U.S. Sen. Rick Santorum (R-Pa.), former Arkansas Gov. Mike Huckabee, U.S. Sen. Ted Cruz (R-Texas), U.S. Sen. Marco Rubio (R-Fla.), retired neurosurgeon Ben Carson, real estate magnate Donald Trump, former Florida Gov. Jeb Bush and others are actively courting this bloc of voters. Unfortunately, more and more of the candidates are relying on incendiary rhetoric and religious division to win support.[6]

Among other things, Americans United for Separation of Church and State has noted that Jeb Bush and Ted Cruz came out in favor

---

6. Rob Boston, "God on the Campaign Trail Months Shy of November, Religious Issues Are Already Roiling the 2016 Presidential Election," *Church and State*, Jan. 2016, featured on *Americans United*, https://www.au.org/church-state/january-2016-church-state/featured/god-on-the-campaign-trail.

of letting refugees into America, but only certain ones: Christians. Ben Carson simply chose to play to fears of "otherness," comparing Syrian refugees to "rabid dogs." Donald Trump, of course, stands alone with the already discussed proposal to ban all Muslims from entering the United States. He has also suggested that Muslims must have special ID cards, darkly adding that "it's all about management ... Our country has no management."[7]

Finally, it is not just security threats that are bringing religion to the fore of right-of-center politics. Particularly during the primary season, the religious Right has become a central political force to which Republican candidates must pay homage if they are to have any chance of winning. The most intense scrutiny takes place in religious forums, which get less press. Here the candidates are often grilled with religious questions. In the National Religious Liberties Conference, attended by Cruz, Huckabee, and Jindal, the forum leader asked Cruz how important it is for the president to believe that Jesus Christ is "the king of the President of the United States." Cruz only slightly dodged the question by stating "any president who doesn't begin every day on his knees isn't fit to be commander-in-chief of this country."[8]

It is worth pausing a moment and contrasting "God on the campaign trail" in 2016 with statements by past American Presidents on the relationship between politics and religion. Note the force with which past leaders communicated their conviction that religious matters and political matters should be kept separate. In addition, one can more easily sense the distance between today's Republican Party and the American tradition of religious freedom.

7. Ibid.

8. Ibid.

In every country and in every age, the priest has been hostile to liberty. He is always in alliance with the despot, abetting his abuses in return for protection to his own.

—*Thomas Jefferson, March 17, 1814*[9]

I could not do otherwise without transcending the limits prescribed by the Constitution for the President and without feeling that I might in some degree disturb the security which religion nowadays enjoys in this county in its complete separation from the political concerns of the General Government.

—*Andrew Jackson, refusing to proclaim a national day of fasting and prayer, 1832*[10]

We all agree that neither the Government nor political parties ought to interfere with religious sects. It is equally true that religious sects ought not to interfere with the Government or with political parties. We believe that the cause of good government and the cause of religion suffer by all such interference.

—*Rutherford B. Hayes, statement as Governor of Ohio, 1875*[11]

9. Thomas Jefferson, letter to Horatio G. Spafford, March 17, 1814, archived by *Founders Online National Archives*, http://founders.archives.gov/documents/Jefferson/03-07-02-0167.

10. Andrew Jackson, letter to the Synod of the Reformed Church, June 12, 1832, *Correspondence of Andrew Jackson*, ed. John Spencer Bassett (Washington, DC: Carnegie Institute of Washington, 1929), 4:447.

11. Rutherford B. Hayes, Opening of 1875 Gubernatorial Campaign speech, Marion, OH, July 31, 1875, archived by *Rutherford B. Hayes Presidential Center*, http://www.rbhayes.org/hayes/content/files/RBHSpeeches/speech_147_opening_of_the_gubernatorial_campaign.htm.

The divorce between Church and State ought to be absolute. It ought to be so absolute that no Church property anywhere, in any state or in the nation, should be exempt from equal taxation; for if you exempt the property of any church organization, to that extent you impose a tax upon the whole community.

—**James A. Garfield, Congressional Record, 1874**[12]

To discriminate against a thoroughly upright citizen because he belongs to some particular church, or because, like Abraham Lincoln, he has not avowed his allegiance to any church, is an outrage against the liberty of conscience, which is one of the foundations of American life.

—**Theodore Roosevelt, 1908 Letter To J. C. Martin**[13]

And I should like to assure you, my Islamic friends, that under the American Constitution, under American tradition, and in American hearts, this Center, this place of worship, is just as welcome as could be a similar edifice of any other religion. Indeed, America would fight with her whole strength for your right to have here your own church and worship according to your own conscience. This concept is indeed a part of America, and without that concept we would be something else than what we are.

—**Dwight Eisenhower, on Muslims in America at Ceremonies Opening the Islamic Center, 1957**[14]

12. James A. Garfield, speaking on the Sundry Civil Appropriation Bill, June 22, 1874, 43rd Congress, 1st session, *Congressional Record*, 5384.

13. Theodore Roosevelt, "Letter to Mr. J. C. Martin Concerning Religion and Politics, November 6, 1908," in *Presidential Addresses and State Papers, November 15, 1907, to November 26, 1908*, vol. 7, 1868.

14. Dwight D. Eisenhower, "Speech at Islamic Center of Washington,"

It is difficult to imagine any of the 2016 Republican primary candidates making any of these statements today without tarnishing their chances to win the Republican nomination.

The Coalition of the Certain

How did we end up with this odd concoction of "freeligion" on the American Right, and what is the relationship between "freeligion" and conservatism? One explanation offered by the public intellectual Andrew Sullivan in his 2006 book *The Conservative Soul: Fundamentalism, Freedom, and the Future of the Right* is that the rise of what he calls the "theoconservatives" solely reflects the rise of religious fundamentalism, and that this fundamentalism is a betrayal of faith as he understands it, and of "true conservatism" as a political philosophy.[15]

Sullivan's portrait of the intersection of fundamentalism and American politics is fascinating as is his heartfelt and contrasting description of his own views on religion and political freedom. But in many ways Sullivan is caught in the same bind as the constitutional lawyer Bruce Fein whom we discussed in chapter 1. Sullivan makes an error similar to Fein's in characterizing his own temperament and philosophy as "conservative" rather than liberal. And, in his precisely backward representation of conservatism, he inadvertently hands rhetorical power to the very conservative and fundamentalist tendencies that he abhors.

June 28, 1957, archived at IIP Digital, *US Embassy*, http://iipdigital.usembassy. gov/st/english/texttrans/2007/06/20070626154822lnkais0.6946985. html#axzz47LFn5STT.

    15. Andrew Sullivan, *The Conservative Soul: Fundamentalism, Freedom, and the Future of the Right* (New York: HarperCollins Publishers, 2006).

Although fundamentalism and authoritarianism are not the same as conservatism, they share an aversion to the uncertainty associated with change. Stated alternatively, a conservative typically has some discomfort with uncertainty, but this is particularly true for the authoritarian or the fundamentalist. By contrast, those who are not conservative tend to be much more open to uncertainty and change—some reveling in uncertainty to a fault.

The basic contours of this distinction are fairly straightforward. For example, the definition of conservatism that Hayek referenced in 1960—"Natural Conservatism … is a disposition averse from change; and it springs partly from a distrust of the unknown"[16]—is from the early twentieth century. This definition is reflected in nearly identical form in a growing body of academic work on conservatism today.[17] This consistency is not an accident. Contrary to what Sullivan implied, you don't need to be a fundamentalist to be averse to uncertainty and change.

On the five big traits that psychologists often use to characterize human personality—openness to experience, conscientiousness, extraversion, agreeableness, and neuroticism—

---

16. Hugh Cecil, *Conservatism* (London: Home University Library, 1912), 9, quoted in Friedrich A. Hayek, *The Constitution of Liberty* (Chicago: University of Chicago Press, 1960), 529.

17. Chris Mooney provides a nice summary of this research in chapter 3 of his book, *The Republican Brain: The Science of Why They Deny Science —and Reality* (Hoboken, NJ: John Wiley and Sons, 2012). The overlap between Hayek's description of conservative temperament and Mooney's research summary is striking. The title of Mooney's book, however, unfortunately belies the extent to which the Republican Party has changed in recent years and that some sincere classic liberals still exist in the GOP (though they lack power).

political liberals rate consistently higher on "openness to experience" whereas political conservatives rate higher on "conscientiousness." Among other things, "openness to experience" corresponds to intellectual flexibility, curiosity, a willingness to entertain new ideas, a toleration of different perspectives and values, and even reveling in change. On the other hand, "conscientiousness" corresponds to being highly goal-oriented, competent, and organized.[18]

"Openness to experience" and "conscientiousness" are positive characteristics, and they are not necessarily mutually exclusive. In an ideal world, one would prefer high scores on both "openness to experience" and "conscientiousness." But directionally, conservatives tend more away from change and uncertainty than toward it. And, within the conservative fold, but further along this continuum of aversion to change and uncertainty, one's outlook tends toward authoritarianism.

Authoritarians are very intolerant of ambiguity, and very inclined toward group-think and distrustful of outsiders (often including racial outsiders). They extol traditional values, are very conventional, submit to established leaders, and don't seem to care much about dissent or civil liberties. They are known for their closed-mindedness, and, indeed, their Manichean view of the world—good and evil, right and wrong, saved and damned, white and black. They have a need for order: Conversely, they can't tolerate uncertainty. In America, they are often religiously conservative fundamentalists who believe the Bible is the unedited word of God.[19]

---

18. Mooney, *The Republican Brain*, chapter 3, "Political Personalities."
19. Ibid.

More than any other characteristic, it may be the relationship to doubt that divides today's American Left and Right. For example, it is not an accident that the prominent liberal financier George Soros named his foundation the Open Society Foundations. He describes an open society as one where "rights are respected, government is accountable, and *no one has a monopoly on the truth.*"[20] Personally, he is described by others as self-critical. He has called his own greatest strength as an investor his ability to quickly change his own mind in the face of new evidence. Like Hayek, Soros admires the twentieth-century philosopher Karl Popper, who emphasized our ongoing and persistent search for "truth" with a lower-case "t"—truth that is always subject to an empirical test.

This philosophy closely resembles that of another prominent liberal entrepreneur and businessman, Elon Musk, founder of Tesla Motors and SpaceX. Describing his approach to business and life, Musk says "I am always to some degree wrong and the aspiration is to be less wrong. We are always to some degree wrong; it does not matter who you are. Trying to minimize the wrongheadedness over time, I believe in that philosophy."[21] The quality of being comfortable with such uncertainty and with such constant questioning and exploration of nuance is very much a *liberal* quality.

Moreover, it is important to note that Sullivan too, in both his stated views and his actions as a writer and blogger, shares these qualities and is liberal in this important respect. What he

20. "George Soros," *Open Society Foundations,* https://www.opensociety foundations.org/people/george-soros my italics.

21. Elon Musk, interview by Rory Cellon-Jones for *BBC,* YouTube video, 18:17, posted by "Singularity Videos," Jan. 13, 2016, https://www.youtube. com/watch?v=SB3eYbPWIvE.

mistakenly labels in his 2006 book as "the conservatism of doubt" much more approximates the temperament and outlook of a liberal. In Hayek's words, "the liberal differs from the conservative in his willingness to face this ignorance and to admit how little we know, without claiming the authority of supernatural sources of knowledge where his reason fails him."[22]

By contrast, the tendency toward an all-encompassing certainty helps explain prominent right-of-center political alliances that at first appear odd or counter-intuitive. Often, the starting point for conservatives is Truth with a capital "T." Their actions and outlook are based on this Truth that has been revealed to them or that they understand instead of truths that may always be subject to tests and uncertainty. This is the nexus between what Soros labels "market fundamentalism" and religious fundamentalism.[23] On the surface, one would think that an economic libertarian and a religious fundamentalist would have absolutely nothing in common. But many economic libertarians tend toward a type of secular fundamentalism. And, the closer one looks, the more often one finds a strong political bond. This bond is rooted in their shared sense of certainty and their purpose or mission.

Consider Charles Koch, the freedom fraud's chief promulgator and perhaps the most influential person in American politics. Koch talks about his own beliefs in the following way: "I'm kind of like Martin Luther when he was on trial, and he said, 'Here I stand, I can do no other.' I dedicate my life to this. These ideas, the ideas we've been talking about, transformed my life, and so it's my mission—I feel a moral obligation to help

---

22. Hayek, *The Constitution of Liberty*, 406.

23. George Soros, "The worst market crisis in 60 years," *The Financial Times*, January 22, 2008, http://www.ft.com/intl/cms/s/0/24f73610-c91e-11dc-9807-000077b07658.html#axzz4C3bvZgGs

other people learn these and transform their lives."[24] In addition, it is instructive that *Forbes* magazine described Charles Koch's 2007 book, *The Secret of Success,* as a text that is "long on hard-edged statements where the author professes an almost Marxist faith in the 'fixed laws' that 'govern human well-being.' His 'Market Based Management' (the term is trademarked), is 'The Science of Human Action.'"[25] For a liberal like Soros, no one has a monopoly on truth. Koch has discovered the Truth, and it is his mission in life to promote it and to battle those who don't understand it.

In this way, it is probably not accidental that Tim Phillips, the person Koch chose to run his extraordinarily influential lobbying group "Americans for Prosperity," attended Jerry Falwell's evangelical Liberty University and was a business partner of Ralph Reed, the Christian Coalition's first executive director and now the director of the Faith and Freedom Coalition. In accepting the position to run Americans for Prosperity, Phillips commented, "I was intrigued by the idea of being able to build a movement based on economic issues, the way that Christian Right folks had built a movement based on social issues."[26]

The common denominator of these two movements was

24. David Rutz, "Charles Koch Responds to 'Dishonest' Harry Reid: 'People Aren't Going to Scare Me Off,'" *Washington Free Beacon*, Nov. 3, 2015, http://freebeacon.com/politics/charles-koch-responds-to-dishonest-harry-reid-people-arent-going-to-scare-me-off/.

25. Daniel Fisher, "Koch's Laws," *Forbes Online*, Feb. 26, 2007, http://www.forbes.com/2007/02/26/science-success-management-lead-ceo-cz_df_0226kochbookreview.html.

26. Jane Mayer, *Dark Money: The Hidden History of the Billionaires behind the Rise of the Radical Right* (New York: Random House, 2016), chapter 6.

more than simply tactics or leading personalities. Closely tied to their affinity for certainty, both Tea Party Republicans and religious fundamentalists tend to be on the extreme end of the conservative temperament, having predominantly authoritarian personalities.[27] In studying authoritarianism, Jonathan Weiler and Marc Hetherington found that among various social characteristics, the strongest single correlation to authoritarianism was viewing the Bible as the literal word of God.[28] But not far behind this social trait was the Tea Party movement itself, which Hetherington has described as "an overwhelmingly authoritarian group of folks."[29] The common element in these movements is clarity and certainty. "If there is one element of the Tea Party that comes through as so clearly authoritarian, it is in the incredibly simple, direct, aggressive understanding of how policy needs to be implemented in this country."[30]

Another key leading member of the "coalition of the certain" is Grover Norquist, whom we discussed briefly in chapter 1. On the one hand, Norquist seems like an unlikely ally of the Christian Right. His longstanding friendship with Ralph Reed, whom he met shortly after college, may simply be a case of the type of strange bedfellows sometimes found in political life. On the other hand, Norquist's monomania to indiscriminately roll back government shares that mission-driven clarity of religious fundamentalism as well as of a secular fundamentalism like

27. See Jonathan Weiler and Marc Hetherington, *Authoritarianism and Polarization in American Politics* (Cambridge, UK: Cambridge University Press, 2009).

28. Jonathan Weiler, audio interview by Chris Mooney for *Point of Inquiry*, Nov. 21, 2011, http://www.pointofinquiry.org/jonathan_weiler_authoritarians_versus_reality/.

29. Quoted in Mooney, *The Republican Brain*, chapter 3.

30. Weiler, *Point of Inquiry* interview.

communism. Indeed, Norquist describes himself as a "market Leninist."

Or, consider the Devos clan from Michigan. The family started and still owns the direct-marketing concern Amway, which in 2012 had more than $11 billion in sales. The Devos clan are religious conservatives and stalwart members of the Koch brothers' donor network. They played an instrumental role in undermining campaign finance laws, including financing the legal challenges that led to the Citizens United decision. As pointed out by Jane Mayer in her book *Dark Money*, the company's business activities are almost entirely fused with "free-enterprise" political zealotry.

> The company's political activism was so unusually intense that one FTC attorney at the time told Forbes, "They're not a business, but some sort of quasi-religious sociopolitical organization." Indeed, as Kim Phillips-Fein writes in *Invisible Hands*, "Amway was much more than a simple direct-marketing firm. It was an organization devoted with missionary zeal to the very idea of free enterprise."[31]

Yet another good example of the "coalition of the certain" is the neoconservative movement of foreign-policy hawks. At the outset, one might ponder why the neoconservatives—whose founding members were New York Jewish intellectuals who began their political journey on the far left—were so at home and influential during the Bush II administration?

The title of Jacob Heilbrunn's empathetic history of neoconservatism—*They Knew They Were Right*—alone is telling. In some of the key elements that Heilbrunn describes, one can see the same extreme tendency toward certainty and a commonality

---

31. Mayer, *Dark Money*, chapter 9.

with religious fundamentalism: "Their self-confidence derives as much from their inherent need to be in opposition, like prophets in the wilderness, as it does from their belief in the rightness of their own ideas."[32] His own experience with neoconservatism is described like this: "I myself was once attracted to neoconservatism. As a teenager and an adult, I found that it supplied me with a beguiling but ultimately artificial clarity about the world that was hard to shake."[33]

Another instructive example is the way in which Hayek's book *The Road to Serfdom* itself is misunderstood within rightwing think tanks—and also, how it is promoted in educational "liberty" seminars for young professionals. In chapter 5, we cover more of the mechanics of how the freedom fraud is promoted and why we easily accept it, but it is worth noting here how the cover of the book *The Road to Serfdom* has changed over the years as the American Right has become more conservative.

When I purchased my copy in 1989, it had been published by the University of Chicago Press in what had become a classic, all-red paperback form. The back of the book contained promotional quotes, including those from more liberal economists such as A. C. Pigou and John Maynard Keynes. Interestingly, the quote from Keynes is particularly supportive: "In my opinion it is a grand book ... Morally and philosophically I find myself in agreement with virtually the whole of it; and not only in agreement with it, but in a deeply moved agreement."

For the freedom fundamentalist, such a quote presents a huge problem. Why would Keynes approve of any part of Hayek's *Road to Serfdom*? Is not Keynes the enemy? Is not Obama's

---

32. Jacob Heilbrunn, *They Knew They Were Right: The Rise of the Neocons* (New York: Anchor Books, 2009), 22.

33. Ibid., 15.

Keynesian stimulus nothing more than a radical, socialist gambit for the government to take over the American economy—a plan to intervene in the economy in a way that would lead to the government intervening in every aspect of our lives?

It should be pointed out that this type of rhetoric is not at the inconsequential fringe of the American Right, but closer to its center. It is the very rhetoric used by past Tea Party stars who increasingly comprise today's Republican leadership. Consider Ted Cruz's comments at an Americans for Prosperity-sponsored Tea Party event in Texas before he became a Senator.

> [Cruz] told the crowd that Obama was "the most radical president ever to occupy the Oval Office" and had hidden from voters a secret agenda—"the government taking over our economy and our lives." Countering Obama, Cruz proclaimed, was "the epic fight of our generation!" As the crowd rose to its feet and cheered, he quoted the defiant words of a Texan at the Alamo: "Victory, or death!"[34]

To support this type of freedom-fraud narrative, one requires black and white simplicity. The old cover of *The Road to Serfdom* failed critically in that respect. The book is now published with two different covers, and neither includes the quote from Keynes. One published version of *The Road to Serfdom* uses instead a single quote from libertarian writer Ronald Bailey: "Nearly half a century ago, most of the smart people sneered when F. A. Hayek published *The Road to Serfdom*. The world was wrong and Hayek was right." Although Hayek's book was indeed controversial when it was first published in 1944, the quote reveals less about the book and much more about the "coalition of the certain"—the tendency toward black and white

---

34. Mayer, *Dark Money*, 181.

clarity, toward their inherent rightness, their sense of embattled isolation, and their need to be in opposition — "like prophets in the wilderness."

The Conservative Animus against Compromise

One of the clearest contrasts between Republican leaders today and those of twenty or thirty years ago is the position taken toward governing and compromise. Today's Republican leaders constantly invoke Reagan as a patron saint and model to emulate, but as noted by Jacob Weisberg, author of the Ronald Reagan volume in the American Presidents series, they act very differently. "Once in office, Reagan said that anytime he could get 70 percent of what he wanted from a legislature, he'd take it. Today's congressional Republicans won't settle even for 99 percent: Their mentality has shifted away from having policies and governing and toward a kind of bitter-end obstructionism."[35] The irony of today's Republicans falling over themselves to assume the mantle of the true Reagan conservative is that Reagan was far more pragmatic and far less conservative. The interesting question is why? What underlying dynamics brought about this change?

Part of the answer to this question—but not the wholly satisfactory answer—is the simple fact that the American Right has become more conservative. Several elements of conservatism that we have already discussed tend directly against compromise. Obviously, if conservatives care more about who is governing than about the policies or principles of governance,

35. Jacob Weisberg, "What Today's Republicans Don't Get about Reagan," *New York Times*, Feb. 24, 2016, http://www.nytimes.com/2016/02/24/opinion/what-todays-republicans-dont-get-about-reagan.html?emc=etal.

there is less room for compromise through policy accommodation. Endlessly compromising on policy won't change the essential discomfort that a conservative might have with a nonconservative opponent who holds power.

Second, pure conservatives struggle with political principles that enable them to work with people whose values differ from their own. "To live and work successfully with others requires more than faithfulness to one's concrete aims. It requires an intellectual commitment to a type of order in which, even on issues which to one are fundamental, others are allowed to pursue different ends."[36] This intellectual commitment is simply not a part of pure conservatism. To the contrary, the escalating competition to be a "real conservative" is measured to a great extent in terms of how committed one is to the concrete aims that conservatives themselves share, and that may not be shared by other Americans. Moreover, compromise itself —an essential feature of American governance—is considered *prima facie* evidence that one lacks conservative credentials. A mainstay of Ted Cruz's and Donald Trump's appeal to the conservative base is precisely their scornful attitude toward compromise. Indeed, the description that Lincoln Chafee offered of President George W. Bush and the conservative base in 2007—"the core still loves that President Bush will never back down or change course or admit error"—very much captures a key dynamic that propels Trump and Cruz today.

Third, the conservative tendency toward certainty discussed above also militates against compromise. There is obviously less reason to compromise if you are certain you are correct— and, in particular, if you are certain that your opponent's alternative views, policies, or priorities will lead to cataclysmic consequences. In many ways, this frame of mind aptly summarizes

---

36. Hayek, *The Constitution of Liberty*, 402.

the conservative response to Obama's efforts to turn the economy around through the Recovery and Reinvestment Act of 2009 and his efforts to slow healthcare inflation and to provide health insurance to more people through the Affordable Care Act of 2010.

As to the Recovery Act, many conservatives were absolutely convinced that mainstream economic analysis was not just incorrect, but disastrously misguided. In particular, they believed that short-term deficit spending on the part of the government in a depressed economy would lead to a counter-productive spike in interest rates, a corresponding reduction in private investment, and an economy that would be weaker still.

With regard to the Affordable Care Act, most conservatives were convinced that it would tragically lead to an increase in healthcare costs and a significant deterioration in the government's financial position as its Medicare and Medicaid obligations would increase with an accelerating rate of healthcare spending. In addition, many conservatives believed that Obamacare would result not only in accelerating healthcare costs, but *fewer* people with health insurance overall.

It should be pointed out, too, that the above claims about the Affordable Care Act, as counter-intuitive and extraordinary as they were given the content of the law, were the *sober* conservative criticisms about the law. Conservative talk radio and Fox News played up the false notion that Obamacare would reduce costs through "death panels." Writing just after the law passed, David Frum observed that "there were leaders who knew better, who would have liked to deal. But they were trapped. Conservative talkers on Fox and talk radio had whipped the Republican voting base into such a frenzy that deal-making was rendered impossible. How do you negotiate with somebody who wants to murder your grandmother? Or —more exactly

—with somebody whom your voters have been persuaded to believe wants to murder their grandmother?"[37]

Frum was correct to point out that some Republican leaders did want to negotiate and that Fox News and conservative talk radio made compromise more difficult, but it would be misleading to think that the difficulty stemmed from conservative populism alone. In terms of overriding certainty, there is now a stark contrast between the American Left and the American Right that is arguably even more clear in political leadership and in intellectual thought.

After the Affordable Care Act became law, we no longer heard much about supposed "death panels"—because none existed—but political leaders and conservative intellectuals continued to be absolutely convinced that the law would implode upon itself, just as many leading conservatives were absolutely convinced that incipient inflation and skyrocketing interest rates were just about to torpedo the American economy.

In a 2013 profile of Yuval Levin, an influential advisor to Paul Ryan and rising intellectual star of the American Right, columnist Jonathan Chait notes the asymmetry in terms of certainty between the proponents of Obama's signature policies and their conservative adversaries.

Even with the data on their side, none of the advocates of Obamacare is nearly as certain the law will succeed as conservatives like Levin are that it will fail. That is a testament only to the overweening ideological certainty that pervades the right. The slowdown in health-care costs is provisional. Perhaps it will peter out, and Obamacare will

---

37. David Frum, "Waterloo," *FrumForum* (blog), March 21, 2010, http://www.frumforum.com/waterloo-page/.

require massive revisions. Perhaps, too, the interest rate
spike Ryan has been warning of will suddenly appear. But
the key thing is that the conservative program since 2009
has hinged on the absolute truth of both these provisions.
The certainty of the imminent debt crisis, and the certainty
that Obamacare would worsen rather than ameliorate it,
undergirded the party's entire strategy. It is not merely the
ideological extremism but Levin's dialectical certainty that
the welfare state will collapse upon itself that has driven
the party's refusal to compromise.[38]

It is worth noting, too, that the Affordable Care Act was not only
designed to make improvements in a number of obvious deficiencies in health law, but it was also designed to win Republican
support. Indeed, as Frum noted when the law passed, "the gap
between this plan and traditional Republican ideas is not very
big. The Obama plan has a broad family resemblance to Mitt
Romney's Massachusetts plan. It builds on ideas developed at
the Heritage Foundation in the early 1990s that formed the basis
for Republican counter-proposals to Clintoncare in 1993–1994."[39]

The similarity to ideas that Republicans had championed
in the past made little difference. Once a narrative of disaster
was established with broad backing from enough think tanks,
political leaders, intellectuals, and popular elements such as
talk radio and Fox News, it was difficult to change course. For
these conservatives, no amount of reform to the health law
—nothing less than total repeal—could avoid the certainty of a
pending calamity. In July of 2013 as the main components of
the law were starting to be implemented, Senator Rand Paul

---

38. Jonathan Chait, "The Facts Are In and Paul Ryan Is Wrong," *New
York Magazine*, May 10, 2013, http://nymag.com/daily/intelligencer/2013/
05/facts-are-in-and-paul-ryan-is-wrong.html.

39. Frum, "Waterloo."

said: "I think that what is going to come out of Obamacare is worse than anybody can imagine. I think it will lead to bankruptcy in the states that are fully embracing it. It will lead to less people having insurance as they find out the insurance is so much more expensive than their current plan."[40]

As we sit here in 2016, circumstances have evolved to a near complete and utter refutation of the certain world view adopted by many conservatives in 2009 and 2010 toward President Obama's signature legislative achievements. Economic Armageddon did not arrive. There was no abrupt interest-rate spike caused by the Recovery Act. To the contrary, even as the economy consistently improved, long-term interest rates stayed below 5%. And, after the Affordable Care Act became law, national healthcare expenditure grew between 3%–5% annually from 2011–2014—the slowest rate in several decades and significantly below the 7% average growth rate during Bush II years.[41] Through 2015, a *net* 20 million people were added to health insurance rolls.[42] Most strikingly, after implementing

40. Rand Paul, interview by Sean Hannity for *Fox News*, Youtube video, 6:04, posted by "Eduardo89rp," July 24, 2013, https://www.youtube.com/watch?v=O-UiSS7YIrM&feature=youtu.be.

41. National Health Expenditure Accounts (NHEA), "Table 01 National Health Expenditures; Aggregate and Per Capita Amounts, Annual Percent Change and Percent Distribution: Selected Calendar Years 1960-2014" (NHE Tables, *Centers for Medicare and Medicaid Services*), last modified Dec. 3, 2015, https://www.cms.gov/Research-Statistics-Data-and-Systems/Statistics-Trends-and-Reports/NationalHealthExpendData/NationalHealthAccountsHistorical.html.

42. Namrata Uberoi, Kenneth Finegold, and Emily Gee, "Health Insurance Coverage and the Affordable Care Act, 2010–2016" (Issue Brief, Office of the Assistant Secretary for Planning and Evaluation, US Department of Health and Human Services), March 3, 2016, https://aspe.hhs.gov/sites/default/files/pdf/187551/ACA2010-2016.pdf.

the law, the federal government's financial picture with respect to healthcare obligations improved to a much greater extent than the architects of the law envisioned. In 2014, the Congressional Budget Office reduced the federal government's 2020 projected healthcare obligation to $70 billion less than the amount forecasted prior to the law's passage.[43]

The toughest part for conservatives in acknowledging these facts is that they fly in the face of the most hardened, cherished belief on the American Right: that the economy is better off when government is inactive, and when there is less of it—in particular the federal government. With both the Recovery Act and the Affordable Care Act, the federal government was acting to address problems. Both pieces of legislation committed more resources in the near term and altered law in order to make the economy and the healthcare marketplace function better in the long term. The certainty on the part of many conservatives that these pieces of legislation were an utter disaster was strongly reinforced by the way laws and policy for many conservatives are often converted to a simplistic moral maxim against government.

---

43. Congressional Budget Office, referenced in "The $900 Billion Slowdown in Federal Health Care Spending," *Committee for a Responsible Federal Budget* (blog), May 6, 2014, http://crfb.org/blogs/900-billion-slowdown-federal-health-care-spending. Per the Congressional Budget Office, "The last pre-ACA CBO baseline was in March 2010 and projected net spending on Medicare and Medicaid at $1.34 trillion in 2020. The April 2014 baseline, though, actually estimates spending on those programs plus the ACA's exchange subsidies in 2020 will be *$70 billion lower than before the ACA was even enacted*, at $1.27 trillion. Note that the most recent comprehensive estimate of the ACA had it increasing federal health spending, on net, by $145 billion in 2020 (including the revenue effect of the exchange subsidies), but that increase has been outdone by the declining projections of federal health spending since then."

"The Best Government Is the Least Government" *as Revealed Truth*

The beginning of this section made the case that *part* of the explanation—*but not the wholly satisfactory answer*—for the bitter-end obstructionism of the American Right today is simply increased conservatism. The reason this answer is not wholly satisfactory is that it raises another question: how did the political leadership of the American Right become so much more conservative? Or, more specifically, why is it that the most conservative elements of the American Right occupy the spotlight while the moderates who display more earnest concern for the principles of a free society and the task of governance lack power? It wasn't always this way. What accounts for the change?

The answer to this lies primarily in the way conservatism has become fused with a simplistic maxim that "the best government is the least government." This simplistic moral maxim trumps political principles and is mistaken as the path to political freedom from which true believers should not stray. There are two important points to understand: 1) why conservatism and this free-market fundamentalism fuse together so well; and, more important, 2) the adverse selection process that is set in motion as conservatives attempt to follow this "true conservatism/freedom" path. This second point gets to the heart of our question above about the increasing extremism and obstructionism of the American Right.

Let's first tackle point one: why conservatism and free-market fundamentalism fuse together so well. In this book's introduction, we noted that Ronald Reagan said in his first inaugural address: "It's not my intention to do away with government. It is rather to make it work—work with us, not over us; to stand by our side, not ride on our back. Government can and must provide opportunity, not smother it; foster productivity, not stifle it." On their own, these words seem hardly recognizable as Reagan's—or at least, our current stereotype of what Reagan believed. Without the giveaway, they sound more like something that Bill Clinton, Al Gore, or Barack Obama might say today. The statement is certainly far removed from the views of influential Republicans today—recall Grover Norquist's ideal of cutting the federal government in half and in half again until it's so small "we can drown it in the bathtub."[44]

How did conservatism move from a more balanced view that government may overreach to the simplified, stridently anti-government view that has become mainstream on the American Right today? In short, why is conservatism susceptible to the freedom fraud? Most good frauds have two common characteristics. First, they build on something that is true or something that has an element of truth to it for plausibility (for example, "the Internet is going to be huge"). Second, they play to something that we want (for example, money, weight loss, youthful appearance).

The element of truth that the freedom fraud builds on is that market forces are indeed powerful. A multitude of private individuals and private corporations freely contracting and acting on price signals can accomplish tasks that are beyond the scope of what any one individual or any small group of planners might accomplish. On the cover of his book *Free to Choose*, the famous University of Chicago economist Milton Friedman is shown holding a pencil. The pencil is provided as an example of a simple device that would be difficult for any one single planner to produce alone. As seemingly simple as it is, a pencil is made of rubber, aluminum, wood, graphite, and paint. For any one individual or individual firm to mine the aluminum

---

44. "Grover Norquist Quotes," *BrainyQuote*, http://www.brainyquote. com/quotes/authors/g/grover_norquist.html.

ore, harvest the wood, process the rubber, etc. in a completely vertically integrated process would be impossible. However, thousands of people and/or hundreds of different private firms working together in coordination through price signals are able to produce pencils cheaply and plentifully. In this way, markets are powerful in a way that is easy to overlook and underappreciate. That is the "magic of the market" as it is sometimes called.

Free-market fundamentalists, however, tend to extend this insight as a kind of revealed Truth that applies to all social interaction. In the real world, those who understand well the virtues of private markets also have an appreciation for how private markets fail: how government is required to establish the rules of the road to make markets work, where government must improve upon what are called "free-rider" problems or pollution problems, or where government should supplant markets entirely for tasks that are far better addressed through organized common effort, such as national defense.

To do all this well requires enlightened, vibrant, and *active* governance. Free-market fundamentalists tend to look past this entirely. As with biblical literalists, their inspiration and authority are drawn from selectively quoted, long-ago texts. Free-market fundamentalists reference writers like Adam Smith or Hayek as authorities who led the way to the revealed truth that others just don't get. Furthermore, like biblical literalists, they tend to look past the sections of those same texts that directly contradict their simplified, moral maxims. For example, among the large and highly influential network of conservative think tanks and lobbying groups that incessantly advocate for "freedom," you may find frequent references to the wisdom of Adam Smith or Hayek, but you probably won't come across the following quote wherein Hayek cites Adam Smith on the manifold and obvious requirements of government:

To create conditions in which competition will be as effective as possible, to supplement it where it cannot be made effective, to provide the services which, in the words of Adam Smith, "though they may be in the highest degree advantageous to a great society, are, however, of such a nature, that the profit could never repay the expense to any individual or small number of individuals"—*these tasks provide, indeed, a wide and unquestioned field of state activity.* In no system that could be rationally defended would the state just do nothing. An effective competitive system needs *an intelligently designed and continuously adjusted legal framework* as much as any other.[45]

This is a difficult pill for a free-market fundamentalist to swallow—in particular the two parts I italicized: 1) the tasks that require a "wide and unquestioned field of state activity" and 2) the need for a persistently active legislative government —an "intelligently designed and continuously adjusted legal framework." The free-market fundamentalist believes just the opposite—that the use of a particular item of property affects only the interests of its owner and that individuals and private firms freely contracting on their own *always* lead to an optimal outcome for society as a whole. For the market fundamentalist, "the best government is the least government" because there is next to nothing that a government can do that is worthwhile.

From this standpoint, we can better understand that conservatives fall for free-market fundamentalism in part because it appeals to something they want: an inactive government that stands against change. If conservative temperament is foremost "a disposition averse from change," as we earlier observed, there

---

45. Hayek, *The Road to Serfdom*, 39; my italics.

is a powerful appeal to the conservative of the false wisdom that the best government is one that is inactive. In this way, "the best government is the least government" is the most potent distillation of the freedom fraud because it tightly joins the "do nothing" statism associated with conservatism to a misguided notion of political freedom.

In addition, we can more fully understand "the bitter-end obstructionism" of the American Right today and the intense animosity toward its political opponents. For starters, if one takes the view that there is next to nothing that a government can do that is worthwhile, then all government activity quickly becomes suspect or nefarious. Some see taxation as a type of theft—to be fought at almost any level. As well, all those who present themselves as working on behalf of the public interest —as either statesmen, public servants, or advocates for the public good—are viewed at best suspiciously, but more often as disingenuous leeches. Rather than letting the "free market" work its magic, these individuals or groups lean on government's authority to rob other people and advance their own agenda.

A conservative/free-market fundamentalist who holds this view is going to be very much estranged from someone who is in government or who wants to work with government to promote the public good. Moreover, to the extent that a legislator holds an intensely skeptical view of what can be constructively accomplished through legislation (beyond lowering taxes and otherwise trying to "roll back" government), that legislator's purpose shifts to a more purely political orientation. His primary purpose simply becomes a political battle with the opposition: those who don't understand the revealed truth of "the best government is the least government" in the way that he does. Ironically, the misguided idealism of "the best government is the least government" tends not toward limited government, but toward unlimited politics because governance itself becomes an afterthought.

Most pundits discuss the partisan division that has increased during Obama's presidency as a division between Democrats and Republicans. But the more interesting dynamic has taken place on the Right between free-market fundamentalists, on the one hand, and the more moderate Republicans who actually believe government can advance the public good. In this way, the key dividing line has been right of center.

At the start of Obama's presidency, the most conservative elements of the Republican Party felt that they had lost the 2008 election because *they had not been conservative enough.* Their adversary was not just Barack Obama, but those RINOs (Republican In Name Only) on the Right who wanted to compromise with Democrats and govern. It was not just Obama who was surprised by the bitter-end obstructionism he increasingly faced as he took office. Moderate Republicans also soon realized they were on the Republican Party's fringe. Steve LaTourette, a long-time moderate Republican congressman from Ohio, indicated to political reporter Jane Mayer that he was astonished when he went to the first meeting of the Republican caucus after Obama was elected.

"When the question came up, about why we lost, these folks were saying, 'It's because we weren't conservative enough.' Well, I looked at the numbers, and we lost 58 percent of the independents!" Yet moderates like himself were getting frozen out. He became so frustrated he eventually retired, becoming a lobbyist and starting an organization aimed at battling the forces of extremism in his party. "I left," he said, "because I was sick of it. I couldn't take it anymore. I was there eighteen years. I understood it

was a contact sport, but whether it was transportation or
student loans, there were things you'd do without thinking. Now you can't get anything done. Some people don't
want the government to do anything," he concluded.[46]

Those politicians who believe in a free society and a constructive role for government find the unchecked conservatism of
the Republican Party increasingly hostile. They are ultimately
weeded out either through primary electoral defeat, general
election loss to a Democrat (after being forced to the Right because of the primary), or simply early retirement in frustration
with the party with which they once identified.

Although this "worst on top" selection process is bad for
governance, it has not necessarily been bad for the Republican
Party over multiple election cycles. As noted in the introduction, with control of the legislative branch and 34 of 50 state
governorships, Republicans are not outliers in terms of political power. Moreover, many in the Republican Party see political moderation as a liability rather than an asset. As House
Freedom Caucus member Raul Labrador recently explained to
the political reporter Ryan Lizza, the GOP in his view does better when it runs on the simple anti-government platform and
dispenses with the notion of governing entirely.

> The problem, in his view, was that the [Republican] Party
> was "governing," he said, adding air quotes to the word.
> "If people just want to 'govern,' which means bringing
> more government, they're always going to choose the
> Democrat."[47]

---

46. Mayer, *Dark Money*, 173.

47. Ryan Lizza, "A House Divided," *New Yorker*, Dec. 14, 2015.

In a way, the Republican Party—and by extension our politics at large—have become trapped by the rhetoric of the freedom fraud. Once one rises to political power by assailing government in general and accusing one's political opponent of being on a crusade to end freedom, then what? Engage in the business of governing and pass a piece of bipartisan legislation? On the Right—and in particular for a *federal* legislator on the Right —that's the path to a well-financed primary challenger and the end of a political career. To the contrary, the political logic of an anti-government party is a kind of nihilistic downward spiral described by former legislative aide Mike Lofgren:

> A couple of years ago a Republican committee staff director told me candidly (and proudly) that there was a method to all this obstruction and disruption. Should Republicans succeed in preventing the Senate from doing its job, it would further lower Congress's favorability rating among the American people. In such a scenario the party that presents itself as programmatically against government—i.e., the Republican Party—will come out the relative winner. As someone who came to Washington believing that it was a privilege to do the public's business on Capitol Hill, I found this admission—or rather, boast, troubling.[48]

In the US Senate and especially in the House of Representatives, there are now very few moderate Republicans—moderate in the sense that their appreciation for the principles of American governance serves to *check* their conservatism, their tendency toward absolute certainty, and their fealty to the freedom fraud.

---

48. Mike Lofgren, *The Party Is Over: How Republicans Went Crazy, Democrats Became Useless, and the Middle Class Got Shafted* (New York: Penguin Books, 2013), 27-28.

The start of this section contrasted the bitter-end obstruction-ism of today's Republicans to Ronald Reagan. In addition to the rising animus against compromise, the increased conservatism and politics of the freedom fraud on the Right help to explain the troubled relationship that today's Republicans have with the empirical world. This difficulty arises most pointedly when facts run counter to cherished beliefs: the subject of chapter 3.

Addendum to Chapter 2:
Uncertainty and Freedom

In chapter 1, we noted that conservatism stands in opposition to the principle of restraint required for the rule of law and for a free society: that conservatives care more about who is governing than about the constraints on those who govern. It is worthwhile to note here briefly how the discussion of certainty and conservatism above provides further insight as to *why* conservatism struggles with the principle of restraint.

A crucial element of the rule of law—the restraint that is required by the rule of law—embraces uncertainty. A prosecutor may "know" that he has found a criminal and the criminal deserves a certain punishment, but under the rule of law, as articulated in the Sixth Amendment in the Bill of Rights, we require that the accused person have a capable defense. Even in cases that may seem obvious, we defer to the established laws, procedures, and precedents because we know our initial judgment may be fallible. In this way, a free society requires the ability to tolerate and live with some level of uncertainty, some benefit of the doubt as to the things we "know" to be true.

This uncertainty also applies to the goodness or the correctness of those who are in government and is exactly why we apply legal restraint to those in power, and why we divide the powers of government. In the words of Judge Learned Hand, "The spirit of liberty is the spirit which is not too sure that it is right." Conservatism tends in a different direction. This tendency toward absolute certainty is why conservatism can have a corrosive effect on principles of liberty, and why it can be absolutely toxic if conservatism is misunderstood as liberty.

Chapter 3

A Lack of Interest in New Ideas and Obscurantism When New Ideas Appear to Threaten Cherished Values

Personally, I find that the most objectionable feature of the conservative attitude is its propensity to reject well-substantiated new knowledge because it dislikes some of the consequences which seem to follow from it—or, to put it bluntly, its obscurantism. I will not deny that scientists as much as others are given to fads and fashions and that we have much reason to be cautious in accepting the conclusions that they draw from their latest theories. But the reasons for our reluctance must themselves be rational and must be kept separate from our regret that the new theories upset our cherished beliefs. I can have little patience with those who oppose, for instance, the theory of evolution or what are called "mechanistic" explanations of the phenomena of life simply because of certain moral consequences which at first seem to follow from these theories, and still less with those who regard it as irreverent or impious to ask certain questions at all. ... Should our moral beliefs really prove to be dependent on factual assumptions shown to be incorrect, it would be hardly moral to defend them by refusing to acknowledge facts.

—F. A. Hayek

In chapter 2, we noted how the strong moralism and the temperament of certainty in conservatism tends against bedrock political principles of a free society such as religious tolerance, the ability to work with people of different moral persuasions, and the ability to compromise. This tension is obscured by the fact that conservatism is often mistaken or promoted as the political philosophy of freedom. Moreover, to the extent that conservatism tends toward free-market fundamentalism in economic affairs, governance and compromise become acutely difficult. Why should one be interested in policy if government should only get out of the way? Why compromise if one is certain that the active governance promoted by one's opponent will only cause harm and destroy liberty?

In a similar way, conservatism tends against another requirement of a free society: an earnest effort to see the world as it is. Of course, we are all subject to strong biases. But the Enlightenment liberalism on which the United States was founded gave primacy to the empirical world and the notion that, whatever our biases are, we share the same set of facts. As John Adams said, "Facts are stubborn things; and whatever may be our wishes, our inclinations, or the dictates of our passion, they cannot alter the state of facts and evidence."[1] In the Declaration of Independence, Jefferson justified the colonies' separation in part on facts "submitted to a candid world," by which he meant an unbiased world. This Enlightenment liberalism was a rejection of the conservatism of the time in which ideas were accepted on authority, faith, or age-old sentiment alone.[2]

This chapter makes the case that conservatism has not changed; it still tends against the empiricism of Enlightenment liberalism. As elegantly stated by Hayek above, it does so most of all when new facts or scientific conclusions (or even long-understood ones) threaten the strong moral positions or cherished

---

1. John Adams, "Argument in Defense of the Soldiers of the Boston Massacre," Boston, MA, December, 1770.

2. Yuval Levin, *Imagining the Future: Science and American Democracy* (New York: Encounter Books, 2008), chapter 6.

beliefs that conservatives hold. The conservative response to this threat is often some form of "obscurantism": the practice of deliberately preventing the facts or the full details of some matter from becoming known.[3] To be clear, in some instances this response is self-deception, but in other instances the response is a deliberate effort to preserve cultural continuity. Since we can't read minds, we'll never know the degree to which conservatives actually convince themselves that empirical evidence is untrue, and the degree to which they cynically cover up inconvenient evidence they privately can't deny.

Conservatism and the Empirical World

A few of the basic features of conservatism that we have already discussed result in a strained relationship with the empirical world. And, as with other principles of a free society that conflict with conservatism, this tension with the empirical world became noticeably acute during the second Bush administration.

First, the conservative emphasis on *who* is in power (discussed in chapter 1) and their *style* of leadership tend to undermine the perceived need for scrutiny as to *what* conservative leadership is doing. The focus on personality or having "decent men in charge" makes the substitution of politics for governance —always a tension—more natural. For the pure conservative, good governance *is* having the right people in charge. As such, the facts that pertain to what that person has done are of secondary importance.

Ron Suskind's profile of George W. Bush's first Treasury Secretary, Paul O'Neill, *The Price of Loyalty*, is perhaps best known for O'Neill's observation that the administration seemed

---

3. "Obscurantism," *Wikipedia*, https://en.wikipedia.org/wiki/Obscurantism.

obsessed with invading Iraq even before the 9/11 attacks.[4] The
book also received widespread attention for O'Neill's conten-
tion that evidence for weapons of mass destruction was never
well-founded. But in some ways, the focus on the Iraq War—
which was top of mind when the book was published in 2004—
distracted from a broader and more important point about the
general way the Bush II administration operated and how
starkly different this was from the two previous Republican
administrations in which O'Neill had served.

Under Nixon and Ford, O'Neill had been accustomed to the
formation of policy that started with "Brandeis Briefs." These
well-researched papers were the basis of a deliberative process
among the President, his senior advisors, and relevant experts
from which decisions were made. During the Bush II administration, this bottom-up process was reversed. Decisions were
made primarily by the President and his closest advisors, and
the surrounding policy apparatus of government was used primarily to sell those decisions. This reversal was reported by a
number of different people who worked in government under
George W. Bush. For example, Jack Goldsmith also noted that
the hallmark of the Bush II administration was the way the
decisions were made by the president or his closest advisors
without "the need to explain, to justify, to convince, to get people on board, to compromise."[5] For O'Neill this type of decision-
making process warped the information on which the Bush II
administration acted. "If you operate in a certain way—by saying this is how I want to justify what I've already decided to do,
and I don't care how you pull it off—you guarantee that you'll
get faulty, one-sided information."[6]

4. Ron Suskind, *The Price of Loyalty: George W. Bush, the White House,
and the Education of Paul O'Neill* (New York: Simon & Schuster, 2004), 75.

5. Goldsmith, *The Terror Presidency*, 249.

6. Ron Suskind, "Faith, Certainty and the Presidency of George W.

What Suskind and O'Neill identified, however, was not just a particular decision-making process, but a different world view as well. First of all, Bush II may have been less concerned with the details of policy because he clearly understood that the source of his power was drawn more from how he presented his personality to a conservative voting base than from how the press or policy world judged his decisions. In 2004, Suskind recalled a conversation with Mark McKinnon, a longtime senior media adviser to Bush, that offered insight into the perceived relationships among Bush, his supporters, and the press. "And you know what they like? They like the way he walks and the way he points, the way he exudes confidence. They have faith in him. And when you attack him for his malaprops, his jumbled syntax, it's good for us. Because you know what those folks don't like? They don't like you!"[7]

More important, Suskind realized early that the Bush II team members thought about their own relationship to the empirical world in a different way with an expansive view of how their actions molded a new reality.

In the summer of 2002, after I had written an article in *Esquire* that the White House didn't like about Bush's former communications director, Karen Hughes, I had a meeting with a senior adviser to Bush. He expressed the White House's displeasure, and then he told me something that at the time I didn't fully comprehend—but which I now believe gets to the very heart of the Bush presidency. The aide said that guys like me were "in what we call the reality-based community," which he defined as people who "believe that solutions emerge from your judicious study

Bush," *New York Times*, Oct.17, 2004, http://www.nytimes.com/2004/10/17/magazine/faith-certainty-and-the-presidency-of-george-w-bush.html?_r=0.

7. Ibid.

of discernible reality." I nodded and murmured something about Enlightenment principles and empiricism. He cut me off. "That's not the way the world really works anymore," he continued. "We're an empire now, and when we act, we create our own reality. And while you're studying that reality—judiciously, as you will—we'll act again, creating other new realities, which you can study too, and that's how things will sort out. We're history's actors ... and you, all of you, will be left to just study what we do."[8]

On one level, this is not a crazy idea. All executives face a tension between the dictates of circumstance and the reality they aspire to bring about through leadership. For example, Steve Jobs of Apple was known for what colleagues called his "reality distortion field," a quality of at once being removed from reality and, at the same time, through the sheer force of his personality, somehow managing to will products into existence on a timeline and/or with characteristics that initially seemed impossible by the more technically savvy experts who surrounded him (the pencil-necked geeks).

But running a country is vastly different from willing an iPhone into existence or running a company. For starters, this grandiose view of the presidency greatly diminishes the role of the press and policy-makers. In many ways, the press and the traditional policy-making world become the antagonists: the pencil-necked geeks trying to restrain the President from leading and creating a new reality.

Moreover, the very idea of having a single personality/leader responsible for the direction of the United States tends directly against the liberal principles on which the country was founded (it is more consistent with imperialism, which we will discuss in chapter 4). For our purposes, the basic point is that conser-

---

8. Ibid.

vatism tends to diminish the value of "the facts on the ground" by ascribing a greater importance to the personality of leadership, and to what can be done through the force of that personality. Recall Lincoln Chafee's observation about George W. Bush from our introduction: "Despite his many hollow words and the myriad failures—from Hurricane Katrina to Iraq to peace in the Middle East—the core still loves that President Bush will never back down or change course or admit error."

Second, this focus on personality is reinforced by the conservative tendency toward certainty that we discussed in chapter 2. Suskind described this tendency as another key feature of how the Bush II administration operated, and how the desire for certitude could conflict with the empirical world.

> Open dialogue, based on facts, is not seen as something of inherent value. It may, in fact, create doubt, which undercuts faith. It could result in a loss of confidence in the decision-maker and, just as important, by the decision-maker. Nothing could be more vital, whether staying on message with the voters or the terrorists or a California congressman in a meeting about one of the world's most nagging problems. As Bush himself has said any number of times on the campaign trail, "By remaining resolute and firm and strong, this world will be peaceful."[9]

Suskind made this observation of the Bush II administration in 2004. What is interesting is how well Suskind's description of the link between the Bush administration's aversion to doubt and to open discussion dovetails with a blog post that captured broad attention across the conservative community in 2010, "Frum, Cocktail Parties, and *the Threat of Doubt*" (my italics). This post was written by Julian Sanchez, a libertarian scholar and senior

---

9. Ibid.

fellow at the CATO Institute. Sanchez's criticism was directed not at any one leader or group, but at the entire conservative media community. The common conservative tendency identified by both Suskind and Sanchez is an inclination to resist new information that might threaten solidarity, confidence, and certainty.

> One of the more striking features of the contemporary conservative movement is the extent to which it has been moving toward epistemic closure. Reality is defined by a multimedia array of interconnected and cross promoting conservative blogs, radio programs, magazines, and of course, Fox News. Whatever conflicts with that reality can be dismissed out of hand because it comes from the liberal media, and is therefore ipso facto not to be trusted. (How do you know they're liberal? Well, they disagree with the conservative media!) This epistemic closure can be a source of solidarity and energy, but it also renders the conservative media ecosystem fragile. Think of the complete panic China's rulers feel about any breaks in their Internet firewall: The more successfully external sources of information have been excluded to date, the more unpredictable the effects of a breach become. Internal criticism is then especially problematic, because it threatens the hermetic seal. It's not just that any particular criticism might have to be taken seriously coming from a fellow conservative. Rather, it's that anything that breaks down the tacit equivalence between "critic of conservatives" and "wicked liberal smear artist" undermines the effectiveness of the entire information filter.[10]

---

10. Julian Sanchez, "Frum, Cocktail Parties, and the Threat of Doubt," *Julian Sanchez* (blog), March 26, 2010, http://www.juliansanchez.com/2010/03/26/frum-cocktail-parties-and-the-threat-of-doubt/.

Finally, beyond an emphasis on the personality of leadership and a general aversion to uncertainty, the most acute tension between conservatism and the empirical world arises when new facts seem to threaten a moral certainty or a cherished belief. The most obvious example, referenced by Hayek at the start of this chapter, is where science collides with biblical literalism, specifically the theory of evolution. This example is hardly novel, nor even the mechanism that motivates the denial of science or of well-understood facts. Indeed, almost echoing the quote from Hayek, the conservative scholar and former policy advisor to George W. Bush, Yuval Levin, acknowledges: "On those issues where the right has a problem with science, it usually arises when science poses some kind of threat to what conservatives see as the imperative of cultural continuity ... an argument about morals and values."[11]

Because biblical literalism has a meaningful presence in the United States on the Left and the Right, it is not surprising that a significant portion of Americans do not believe that humans evolved over time. For example, a 2013 Pew Research survey found that 30% of Democrats and 28% of Independents reject evolution entirely and believe that humans have existed in their present form since the beginning. For Republicans, however, the number is much higher at 48%.[12] Moreover, it is much more common to find conservative intellectuals and conservative leadership defending the teaching of "alternative

---

11. Jeremy Manier, "Coyne and Levin, Pt. 2," *Science Life* (University of Chicago Medicine and Biological Sciences), April 9, 2009, https://sciencelife. uchospitals.edu/2009/04/09/coyne-and-levin-pt-2/.

12. "Public's Views on Human Evolution," Religion and Public Life, *Pew Research Center*, Dec. 30, 2013, http://www.pewforum.org/2013/12/30/ publics-views-on-human-evolution/?utm_medium=App.net&utm_ source=PourOver.

science" and/or injecting their perceived religious conflicts with science into politics. For example, Levin said:

> I would want my children to be taught the facts of evolution, but I am not troubled if my neighbor would rather that his children were taught a different kind of story of origins addressed to a different realm of human knowledge, with a different point to make. Nothing crucially common to us is lost or damaged when we make these choices; and nothing about being an American requires one to know a particular set of facts about natural history ...[13]

Low-key tone aside, this is a fairly remarkable statement by a person considered to be a thought leader of the American Right —and made in a book about science and democracy no less. The statement implies that nothing is lost to us by teaching "facts" we now understand as false and presenting them as natural history.[14] Levin's view starkly contrasts with Hayek's admonition that our views of science and facts need to be rational and should be kept separate from the perceived threat to morals or cherished beliefs.

---

13. Levin, *Imagining the Future*, 226.

14. To be sure, Levin in other interviews and writings sometimes presents his case against an overreach of science only where it becomes the sole avenue to understand morality and humanity. Indeed, in the continuation of the quote above, he makes this second argument as well: "let alone to accept the dubious proposition that scientific knowledge is the only knowledge relevant to the question of human beginnings, and so of human nature." Above, I present the first statement without the second because they are indeed two different arguments. The "overreach" argument appears to me to be a straw-man position, but it is certainly a more defensible, reasonable position. However, he seems to meander between the two, at best. At any rate, the statement above condoning a different type of natural history is very clear.

Among conservative politicians, it is not hard to encounter a much more aggressive stance against science when science appears to threaten conservative religious beliefs. Former Congressman Paul Broun, who was a member of the Tea Party Caucus and also a member of the House Committee on Science, Space, and Technology, stated in 2012 that "all that stuff I was taught about evolution and embryology and Big Bang theory, all lies straight from the Pit of Hell... lies to try to keep me and all the folks who are taught that from understanding that they need a savior."[15] Congressman Broun is also known for his view that "Earth is about 9,000 years old," and that "it was created in six days as we know them." These statements would be remarkable enough coming from a member of the US Congress—let alone a medical doctor chosen by Republican leadership to serve on the House Committee on Science, Space, and Technology. The important point is the manner in which he rejects science as a perceived threat to a cherished belief.

Faith and spirituality need not lead to a conflict with the empirical world. The tension arises with conservatism and its tendency toward certainty, and not necessarily religiosity. The distinction here is perhaps best illustrated by a conversation that Suskind had with Jim Wallis, a pastor who had a brief working relationship with George W. Bush at the start of his presidency.

> "Faith can cut in so many ways," he said. "If you're penitent and not triumphal, it can move us to repentance and accountability and help us reach for something higher than ourselves ... But when it's designed to certify our righteousness—that can be a dangerous thing. Then it pushes self-criticism aside. There's no reflection. Where people often

15. "House Science Panel Wears Blinders," Opinion, *Statesman*, Jan. 9, 2013, http://www.statesman.com/news/news/opinion/house-science-panel-sees-no-climate-change/nTrM2/.

get lost is on this very point," he said after a moment of thought. "Real faith, you see, leads us to deeper reflection and not—not ever—to the thing we as humans so very much want." And what is that? "Easy certainty."[16]

The Triad of Obscurantism

To the extent that conservatism tends toward free-market fundamentalism in economic affairs, the power and expanse of this obscurantism is greatly magnified. The reason is that facts need to correspond to the ideal that less government or inactive government is always better. The belief system creates a much larger chasm with the daily realities of political economy. If the empirical world suggests otherwise, then market fundamentalists must obscure the facts that threaten their belief that "the best government is the least government."

Alone, this free-market fundamentalism would probably not be potent. But it does not function alone. Here we introduce a critical partner in the promotion of the freedom fraud: large corporate interests that pollute, engage in fraud, or otherwise benefit greatly from weak or inactive governance (Big Tobacco and the US fossil-fuel industry in particular).

Overall, we can best understand the very intense force of obscurantism now on the American Right by considering it in three parts—voices, funders, voters—that are reinforcing:

- **Voices**—the thought leadership of free-market fundamentalism, including think tanks, advocacy groups, and politicians

---

16. Suskind, "Faith, Certainty and the Presidency of George W. Bush."

- **Funders**—the corporations and special interests that stand to gain the most from inactive governance

- **Voters**—a conservative voting base that has become more concentrated on the American Right

The issue of global warming provides a vivid illustration of how these three complementary forces interact. For starters, it's hard to read the Hayek quote that begins this chapter and not think of global warming. Hostility to the theory of global warming and to science in general has mirrored the ascent of the Republican Party's most conservative elements. The defensive nature of a tweet by Jon Huntsman in his effort to be the moderate choice for the 2012 Republican presidential nominee speaks volumes: "To be clear. I believe in evolution and trust scientists on global warming. Call me crazy."[17]

Hayek perfectly captures the manner in which contemporary conservative opposition to climate science arises. James Inhofe, the US Senate's most outspoken critic of the science on climate, said, "If you regulate carbon, you regulate life ... that's in my opinion what it is all about."[18] For conservative temperament, concerns over the theory's *consequences* to a "way of life" —however ill-founded—drive the view of science and stand at the heart of the debate.

Clearly, the *most* conservative elements of the Republican Party—in particular Tea Party Republicans—are the most opposed to addressing the problem with a government remedy and

17. Jon Huntsman, Twitter post, Aug. 18, 2011, https://twitter.com/JonHuntsman/status/104250677051654144.

18. James Inhofe, interview by Rachel Maddow, *Rachel Maddow Show*, MSNBC, March 15, 2012.

who have the most difficulty with the facts of climate science. For example, a recent survey by the Center for Climate Change Communication at George Mason University shows that more than 70% of liberal and moderate Republicans favor regulating carbon dioxide as a pollutant compared to just 36% of Tea Party Republicans.[19]

For the Tea Party Republican and the ardently committed free-market fundamentalist, there is a logic to their denial and obscurantism. In a 2007 speech to the Royal Economic Society, the British Economist Sir Nicholas Stern famously described global warming as "the greatest market failure the world has seen." He made the simple point that "those who damage others by emitting greenhouse gases generally do not pay."[20] In other words, greenhouse gases are a corruption of property and in failing to address this, the market does not work perfectly. In this instance, active governance may enable a market economy to perform better (internalizing the cost of the "externality,"[21] in the words of a modern economist) thus improving upon a corruption in property—and reinforcing liberty. Or, as Ronald Reagan more eloquently summarized the concept in 1988, "many laws protecting environmental quality have promoted liberty by securing property against the destructive trespass of pollution."[22]

19. David Roberts, "The GOP Is the World's Only Major Climate-Denialist Party. But Why?" Energy and Environment, *Vox*, Dec. 2, 2015, http://www.vox.com/2015/12/2/9836566/republican-climate-denial-why.

20. Alison Benjamin, "Stern: Climate Change a 'Market Failure,'" *Guardian*, Nov. 29, 2007, http://www.theguardian.com/environment/2007/nov/29/climatechange.carbonemissions.

21. Campbell R. McConnell and Stanely L. Brue and Sean M. Flynn, *Economics: Principles, Problems, and Policies* (New York: McGraw-Hill Irwin, 2009), 335.

22. Ronald Reagan, "Message to the Congress Transmitting the Report

Reagan, of course, was not an environmentalist. But as shown earlier in this book, he was far more pragmatic than are most of today's Republicans. He was concerned about government over-reach, but at the same time he did not want to *eliminate* the Environmental Protection Agency. Moreover, his administration had some environmental accomplishments. Reagan signed the Montreal Protocol, a global treaty that phased out numerous substances responsible for depleting our atmospheric ozone layer. In this way, he was not a free-market fundamentalist.

The voice of today's American Right is very much driven by free-market fundamentalism (when it supports conservative ends). And, if you believe that markets are infallible and that government should always be inactive as a kind of revealed Truth, then you will indeed have a tough time accepting *"the greatest market failure the world has seen."* For the vast majority of publishing climate scientists and respected scientific societies,[23] global warming is a direct threat to the relatively stable climate in which human civilization advanced over the past 10,000 years. For free-market fundamentalists, global warming directly threatens their world view in very much the same way that evolution threatens the biblical literalist. The response to this threat is to obscure or deny facts that don't fit their world view.

In their excellent book, *Merchants of Doubt*, Naomi Oreskes and Erik Conway show that the earliest prominent scientists to argue against climate science were typically fierce anti-communists and hardened Cold Warriors who regarded science as a critical instrument in the fight against communism. As with free-market fundamentalists, they viewed any regulation as

of the Council on Environmental Quality," Washington, DC, Oct. 3, 1988.

23. "Scientific Consensus: Earth's Climate Is Warming," Global Climate Change: Vital Signs of the Planet, *NASA*, http://climate.nasa.gov/scientific-consensus/.

the denial of liberty and a slippery slope to communism. For these scientists, the intense effort to present a different set of facts on climate followed a similar pattern of denying and obscuring facts on a range of other issues.

> Fred Singer gave his game away when he denied the reality of the ozone hole, suggesting that people involved in the issue "probably [have] ... hidden agendas of their own—not just to 'save the environment' but to change our economic system ... some of these 'coercive utopians' are socialists, some are technology-hating Luddites; most have a great desire to regulate—on as large a scale as possible." He revealed a similar anxiety in his defense of secondhand smoke: "If we do not carefully delineate the government's role in regulating [danger] ... there is essentially no limit to how much government can ultimately control our lives." Today tobacco, tomorrow the Bill of Rights.[24]

As shown by Oreskes and Conway, the playbook for fighting laws that might curb carbon pollution was lifted directly from the playbook developed by the public relations firm Hill & Knowlton to fight tobacco regulation on behalf of Big Tobacco. This playbook used the inherent uncertainty of the scientific method against itself.

> Doubt is crucial to science—in the version we call curiosity or healthy skepticism, it drives science forward—but it also makes science vulnerable to misrepresentation, because it is easy to take uncertainties out of context and

---

24. Naomi Oreskes and Erik M. Conway, *Merchants of Doubt: How a Handful of Scientists Obscured the Truth on Issues from Tobacco Smoke to Global Warming* (New York: Bloomsbury Press, 2010), 249.

create the impression that *everything* is unresolved. This was the tobacco industry's key insight: that you could use *normal* scientific uncertainty to undermine the status of actual scientific knowledge ... "Doubt is our product," ran the infamous memo written by a tobacco industry executive in 1969, "since it is the best means of competing with the 'body of fact' that exists in the minds of the general public." The industry defended its primary product—tobacco—by manufacturing something else: doubt about its harm. "No proof" became a mantra that they would use again in the 1990s when attention turned to secondhand smoke. It also became the mantra of nearly every campaign in the last quarter of a century to fight facts.[25]

This strategy was enormously successful with the general public, as Oreskes and Conway convincingly document. However, it's useful to think of it in the context of our previous discussion of conservatism's aversion to uncertainty. We can see how this strategy would be particularly effective with conservatives, and with free-market fundamentalists.

The free-market fundamentalist is weighing, on the one hand, the certainty of a market interference that is bad almost by definition—and may very well lead to tyranny—with, on the other hand, a threat to human health or the environment around which *some* voices are uncertain. From this perspective, the decision is a no-brainer. The conservative is generally faced with the same tradeoff, though it may not be regarded in such stark terms as in the case of the free-market fundamentalist.

In addition, to the extent that the facts of a market failure become obvious and/or difficult to ignore, one predictable response from the voice of free-market fundamentalism is to amp

25. Ibid., 34.

up the perceived certainty of the dire consequences surrounding
the proposed government remedy. For example, in 2014 as the
evidence and consequences of a warming planet became more
plainly apparent and as support grew for regulating carbon
emissions in the power sector under the Clean Air Act (even
among some utilities), the warnings over the consequences of
regulating carbon only became more shrill. Here's how Charles
Krauthammer recently described the EPA threat on Fox News:

> And the story that was missed among all the scandals that
> are supposedly undoing [Obama's] presidency is the cli-
> mate change regulations ... You want to run America? Don't
> run for the presidency, get yourself appointed head of the
> E.P.A. It makes Stalin's five-year plans look like a picnic the
> way they're going to have control of the economy.[26]

From this vantage point, we can also start to see how the three
legs of the triad of obscurantism complement one another so
well. For leg one—the voices of free-market fundamentalists
—there is a clarity of purpose and mission in addition to the
allure of cash. Their sense of mission is reinforced by the crusade against all manner of active governance at the same time
as their cash needs are met by the second leg of the triad: the
funders who provide the financial support for the voice of market fundamentalism.

The funders are generally corporations with a strong vested
interest in obscuring facts associated with the products they
sell, or companies that otherwise benefit from inactive/weak

26. Charles Krauthammer, "Obama Operating Under His Own Constitution, 'Ruling Like A Banana Republic,'" *Real Clear Politics*, June 12, 2014,
http://www.realclearpolitics.com/video/2014/06/12/krauthammer_
obama_operating_under_his_own_constitution_ruling_like_a_banana_
republic.html.

governance. Even though the funders are among the largest and most profitable corporations in the United States, they benefit greatly from their transactions with the free-market fundamentalist. The influence they can wield in government is vastly increased (or the cost required to pay for that influence is greatly reduced) if their corporate interest is packaged as a philosophy of freedom.

This freedom fraud of inactive governance is sold to and supported by an increasingly conservative base of voters on the American Right. Since these conservatives generally resist change, they are a natural audience for the notion that an active federal government gravely threatens their way of life.

The reinforcing nature of these three forces has been powerful. We now know that while Exxon was funding organizations that zealously undermined the science of climate, its own scientists, who had long concluded that the impacts of global warming were real, were studying how a warming planet would affect their own Arctic drilling operations.[27] We now have cruise ships planning tours through the Northwest Passage, a development unthinkable just decades earlier and simply not possible without a warming planet. And, despite this, and indeed almost a full decade after John McCain strongly supported a cap-and-trade system as a way of reducing carbon pollution, the American Right finds it very difficult to acknowledge that climate change poses a problem. It's even harder to discuss a consequential remedy. Indeed, the normally staid conservative columnist David Brooks recently stated that on the issue of global warming

> the G.O.P. has come to resemble a Soviet dictatorship—a
> vast majority of Republican politicians can't publicly say

----

27. Neela Banerjee, Lisa Song, and David Hasemyer, "Exxon: The Road Not Taken," *Inside Climate News*, Sept. 16, 2015, http://insideclimatenews. org/content/Exxon-The-Road-Not-Taken.

what they know about the truth of climate change because they're afraid the thought police will knock on their door and drag them off to an AM radio interrogation.[28]

In citing "the vast majority," Brooks probably exaggerates the number of Republican politicians who privately accept climate science, but he is not incorrect in the difficulty of acknowledging facts on this issue for those on the Right who understand the problem and want to do something about it. Of course, the consequences of this "triad of obscurantism" are much greater than the issue of global warming alone. But this single issue does illustrate well the tension between conservatism and the empirical world, how this tension leads to obscurantism, and how this obscurantism has become greatly amplified as conservatism has embraced free-market fundamentalism in economic affairs.

In the next chapter, we will see how some of the same characteristics of conservative temperament relate to anti-internationalism and, paradoxically, to imperialism.

---

28. David Brooks, "The Green Tech Solution," Opinion Pages, *New York Times*, Dec. 1, 2015, http://www.nytimes.com/2015/12/01/opinion/the-green-tech-solution.html?action=click&pgtype=Homepage&clickSource=story-heading&module=opinion-c-col-left-region&region=opinion-c-col-left-region&WT.nav=opinion-c-col-left-region&_r=1.

Chapter 4

A Tendency toward Imperialism

Connected with the conservative distrust of the new and the strange is its hostility to internationalism and its proneness to a strident nationalism ... Only at first does it seem paradoxical that the anti-internationalism of the conservative is so frequently associated with imperialism. But the more a person dislikes the strange and thinks his own ways superior, the more he tends to regard it as his mission to "civilize" others—not by the voluntary and unhampered intercourse which the liberal favors, but by bringing them the blessings of efficient government.

—F. A. Hayek

Our discussion in chapter 1 began with the insight that conservatives care more about who is governing than about constraints on those who govern. We also showed how this conservative aversion to legal restraint domestically was greatly amplified in international affairs, manifesting as a general contempt for treaties and international law. Of course, our constitution wisely sets a higher threshold of a two-thirds majority in the Senate to establish laws that bind us to other nations —whom we know less well—than the threshold to establish laws that effectively bind us to ourselves. But the pure conservative, in his inherent distrust of otherness and aversion to restraint, tends to regard international treaties or laws as a near impossibility and/or almost always folly.

We began our discussion of the strong moral certainty of conservatives and their tendency to divide the world in starkly black and white terms—good/evil, friend/foe, "with us or against us"—in chapter 2. Considered together, we can now see how the attributes of conservatism in chapter 1 and chapter 2 are reinforcing. To the extent that "not us" is inherently untrustworthy or evil, entering into a treaty and/or compromising on a law may itself be regarded as a moral failing for the pure conservative. And, to the extent that such a coexistence is seen as intolerable, the result tends toward a single remaining choice: to conquer ("to win!").

How this insight applies to current Republican politics is in some ways plainly obvious. Since 2008, a rising tide of jingoism playing to fears of otherness on the American Right has corresponded to a more imperialistic approach to foreign affairs (more militaristic and more outwardly directed). Dave Roberts of Vox aptly summarized the foreign-policy discussion of the December 15 Republican primary presidential debate when he declared, "Not only did the GOP learn nothing from Iraq, it seems to know LESS now than it knew then."[1] And, consistent with Hayek's insight above, it stands to reason that Donald Trump—who rose to prominence raising questions about President Obama's birthplace, legitimacy to serve, and intent as a "foreigner" to do harm to the United States—also has the most overtly imperialistic foreign policy of any presidential candidate in recent memory (advocating the forcible seizure of Mideast oil, among other things).

But the more important question is: how did we get here? The Republican Party was not always so uniformly militaristic in its approach to foreign affairs (in the Republican primary race, Senator Rand Paul was the exception that proved the rule among leading candidates). We can understand what hap-

---

1. David Roberts, Twitter post, Dec. 15, 2015, https://twitter.com/drvox/status/676962254416420865.

pened by marking a clear distinction between conservatism by temperament and liberal principles that are conflated with conservatism.

Moral Certainty, Exceptionalism, and Imperialism

The concept of "American exceptionalism" often enters the discussion of US foreign affairs. And there is no doubt that America's founders and prominent leaders throughout its history have viewed America as having a special role in spreading liberty and democracy around the world. America's "cause is the cause of all mankind," said Benjamin Franklin; "We have the power to begin the world over again," insisted Tom Paine; Abraham Lincoln declared America to be "the world's last best hope."[2] But in terms of foreign policy and our *military*, what does American exceptionalism mean in the context of spreading liberty?

In many respects, the founding fathers could not have been more clear. In his farewell address in 1796, George Washington, our nation's greatest warrior, advised future generations to

> avoid the necessity of those overgrown military establishments which, under any form of government, are inauspicious to liberty, and which are to be regarded as particularly hostile to republican liberty.[3]

2. Owen Harries, "The Perils of Hegemony," *American Conservative*, June 21, 2004, http://www.theamericanconservative.com/articles/the-perils-of-hegemony/.

3. George Washington, "Washington's Farewell Address 1796," archived by The Avalon Project: Documents in Law, History and Diplomacy, *Yale Law School*, http://avalon.law.yale.edu/18th_century/washing.asp.

Twenty-five years later, on July 4, John Quincy Adams as Secretary of State gave a historic address after reading the Declaration of Independence, wherein he famously stated that America "goes not abroad in search of monsters to destroy." This short phrase frequently comes up in debates about American foreign policy, but it is worth considering the larger passage from which it is taken to appreciate the force and conviction of his statement.

[America] has, in the lapse of nearly half a century, without a single exception, respected the independence of other nations, while asserting and maintaining her own. She has abstained from interference in the concerns of others, even when the conflict has been for principles to which she clings, as to the last vital drop that visits the heart. ... Wherever the standard of freedom and independence has been or shall be unfurled, there will her heart, her benedictions and her prayers be. But she goes not abroad in search of monsters to destroy. She is the well-wisher to the freedom and independence of all. She is the champion and vindicator only of her own. She will recommend the general cause, by the countenance of her voice, and the benignant sympathy of her example.[4]

Moreover, Washington's quote and John Quincy Adams's statement above should be considered together. The warning against military adventurism abroad is not simply a "realist" argument about the efficacy of exporting democracy and liberty over the barrel of a gun, but a wise wariness of the deleterious effect

---

4. John Quincy Adams, "She Goes Not Abroad in Search of Monsters to Destroy," July 4, 1821, reprinted by *Repository*, July 4, 2013, http://www.theamericanconservative.com/repository/she-goes-not-abroad-in-search-of-monsters-to-destroy/.

that an overgrown military and war has on liberty at home. It is with great irony that some of today's leading neoconservatives, who are among the most enthusiastic proponents of greatly expanding the size of our already dominant military and using that military might aggressively to export "freedom" through war, invoke Alexis de Tocqueville to support their broad view of the world.

To be sure, on domestic-policy issues, Tocqueville's famous and expansive book *Democracy in America* is almost notorious for offering support for positions of both the American Right and the American Left. For example, Tocqueville warned of excessive welfare in "perpetual ameliorations" but also warned of a new aristocracy created from manufacturing and the deleterious impact of the division of labor on the general citizenry. However, on the threat that the military and war pose to liberty, he could not have been more clear.

> No protracted war can fail to endanger the freedom of a democratic country. ... [War] must almost compulsorily concentrate the direction of all men and the management of all things in the hands of the administration. If it does not lead to despotism by sudden violence, it prepares men for it more gently by their habits. All those who seek to destroy the liberties of a democratic nation ought to know that war is the surest and shortest means to accomplish it. This is the first axiom of the science.[5]

To the extent that one regards George Washington, John Quincy Adams, and Alexis de Tocqueville as earnest messengers of the principles of a free society, the idea of American exceptionalism

5. Alexis de Tocqueville, *Democracy in America*, edited by Phillips Bradley and Francis Bowen (New York: Alfred A. Knopf, 1980), vol. 2, 284.

is clearly grounded in the *example* that America should set —
and foremost in setting this example is the restrained and judicious use of its military for defensive purposes. In the context
of Hayek's insight above about conservatism and imperialism,
however, one can easily see how the notion that America is "exceptional" can quickly be perverted to mean just the opposite:
the more one believes "his own ways superior"—(*exceptional*) —
"the more he tends to regard it as his mission to 'civilize' others
—not by the voluntary and unhampered intercourse which the
liberal favors, but by bringing them the blessings of efficient
government."

In this context, we can easily see how an earnest understanding of a free society's principles may lead in one direction
whereas conservative temperament may lead in just the opposite. Until recently, the American Right harbored both foreign-
policy traditions—evident in the American Right's very different responses to the end of the Cold War, Saddam Hussein's
invasion of Kuwait, the September 11 attacks, and the aftermath of the second Iraq war in which no weapons of mass destruction were found. But much in the same way that there was
once a tradition of fiscal restraint that gave way to the chimera
of supply-side economics, there was once a right-of-center
school of thought favoring restraint and multilateralism in international affairs that has now given way to a new notion that
"serious" foreign policy must mean expansive and virtually unrestrained use of our military on nearly all occasions (in particular *if* the military adventurism—like unrestrained fiscal
spending—is led by a conservative). In his thirty years as a staffer in Congress, Mike Lofgren became increasingly dismayed by
the increased militancy—and deference to the military—on
both sides of the political aisle, but particularly in the Republican Party.

While the me-too Democrats have set a horrible example of late of keeping up with the Joneses when it comes to waging war, they cannot hope to match the GOP in their libidinous enthusiasm for invading other countries. John McCain went so far as to propose that we mix it up with Russia—a nuclear armed state!—during its conflict with Georgia in 2008 (remember "we are all Georgians now," a slogan that did not, fortunately, catch on), and Lindsey Graham has been relentlessly agitating for attacks on Iran and intervention in Syria.[6]

Lofgren made these comments in 2012. As mentioned in chapter 1, John McCain's foreign-policy rhetoric is now comparatively dovish next to that of Donald Trump and Ted Cruz. His willingness to stand by the Geneva Conventions and his deference to rules of engagement that currently define war crimes put him among the "politically correct" who stand in the way of America defeating its enemies.

Moreover, although Lofgren's passion and flair sometimes verge on hyperbole, his cultural observation on the extreme deference that we now hold toward military leaders merits close consideration. "Republicans, in their statement on military policy, have taken to making a ritual genuflection to the notion that our elected leaders should follow the advice of military commanders."[7] In the context of our now decade-plus-long "war on terror" and Tocqueville's warning that if war "does not lead to despotism by sudden violence, it prepares men for it more gently by their habits," this cultural shift seems tremendously relevant. Lofgren's observations on this point are worth quoting at length.

------

6. Lofgren, *The Party Is Over*, 98.

7. Ibid.

The GOP seems to have forgotten—even more so than the Democrats, who periodically become enamored of a Wesley Clark or an Eric Shinseki—that our constitutional system of government absolutely and unconditionally requires civilian control of the military. That George Washington faced down his mutinous officers at Newburgh, New York, stands as one of the lesser-known milestones in the development of American self-government. If only it were studied more frequently. Washington's rationale was that the army should not be allowed to overthrow or overawe the republic's properly established magistrates, else a militarized despotism would reign. This was the position of our first president, revered now in ritual as the father of his country but little remembered for his supreme accomplishment: saving the very idea of a self-governing republic. Had Civil War policy been left in the hands of a George McClellan or an Ambrose Burnside, rather than the duly elected president, Abraham Lincoln, a disaster would have resulted that would most likely have left the country cleaved in two. Franklin Roosevelt's mostly political decision to invade North Africa in November 1942 turned out to be a good call. Harry Truman wisely fired General Douglas MacArthur and prevented a bloody and nasty Korean War from becoming a world conflagration. President Kennedy's rejection of his generals' near unanimous advice to invade Cuba may have prevented a nuclear war with the Soviet Union. But for all of Lyndon Johnson's domestic accomplishments, a second term was foreclosed to him because he listened to General William Westmoreland's fantasies of an imminently achievable victory in Vietnam. How have we forgotten all of this?[8]

---

8. Ibid., 98–99.

Returning to the question of how we arrived at this point, the schism in thought leadership of the American Right since the end of the Cold War is perhaps best personified by Owen Harries on the one hand, and Irving Kristol (and his son William Kristol), on the other. As noted by the scholar Jacob Heilbrunn, Harries became the first John M. Olin Fellow in 1984 at the conservative Heritage Foundation, where he wrote numerous articles on foreign affairs and made a name for himself in Washington. He founded, together with Irving Kristol, *National Interest*, which became the first Washington-based neoconservative foreign-policy vehicle.[9]

In the aftermath of the Cold War, Harries's own view on the need for US military might and the extent it should be outwardly employed changed to reflect the Soviet Union's collapse. For Harries, the change from a so-called "bipolar" world to a "unipolar" world, where the United States was the clear leader in economic and military might, increased the need for the United States to act with restraint and in concert with allies in foreign affairs. Heilbrunn said Harries:

> used his magazine to battle the neoconservatives and argue for a more restrained US foreign policy. He felt that the United States was running amok without another superpower to check its worst impulses. It is precisely his belief in the perfidy of communism that prompts him to reject the analogy today between the fight against Islamic terrorism and the cold war: "I think it's to belittle the historical experiences of World War II, not to speak of the Cold War, to equate the terrorists of today and the damage they're capable of with the totalitarian regimes of the previous century."[10]

---

9. Heilbrunn, *They Knew They Were Right*, chapter 3.

10. Ibid.

Moreover, the tack taken by Harries at the end of the Cold War was not unusual on the American Right at the time. In recent writings, Harries has pointed out that even Jeane Kirkpatrick, who had herself been a dedicated Cold Warrior, was expressing a widely held view when she wrote in 1990:

> The United States performed heroically in a time when heroism was required; altruistically during the long years when freedom was endangered. The time when Americans should bear such unusual burdens is past. With a return to "normal" times, we can again become a normal nation—and take care of pressing problems of education, family, industry and technology. It is time to give up the dubious benefits of superpower status and become again an open American republic.[11]

In addition, it is important to note that although today's "neoconservatives" like to describe their own positions as "Reaganite," Reagan departed sharply from neoconservatives in his second term. Neoconservatives had persistently argued that Soviet strength was underestimated, that it was a grave, growing threat that could be countered only with force: ever larger, outwardly directed US military might. Implicit in their view was the notion that negotiating with the Soviets was an impossibility/sheer folly. By the mid 1980s, this certain view of the world was utterly at odds with the reality of an increasingly conciliatory Soviet Union that was in fact crumbling from within. The neoconservatives had great difficulty seeing this change. They were apoplectic when Reagan began negotiating with Gorbachev on eliminating intermediate-range nuclear weapons in Europe, and even more surprised when Gorbachev

---

11. Quoted in Harries, "The Perils of Hegemony."

accepted Reagan's zero intermediate-range nuclear weapons proposal in the spring of 1987.[12] Heilbrunn wrote:

> In May 1988 Reagan visited Moscow for another summit with Gorbachev and stated that the Soviet Union was no longer an evil empire: "No, I was talking about another time, another era." Not the neoconservatives. Reagan was accused of selling out to the communists, of appeasement, of willful naïveté. [The neoconservative Norman] Podhoretz, like James Burnham a generation earlier, was hypnotized by the communist threat. He could not recognize that America's long, vigilant policy of containment had succeeded, much as George F. Kennan had predicted it would. By damming up the Soviet Union at "every nook and cranny," as Kennan had proposed, the United States had caused the Soviet empire to crumble from within. Yet even as it came crashing down, Podhoretz and others maintained that the edifice remained impervious. They had invested too much emotionally in the Soviet Union to conceive that it might disappear. It was their mental balustrade, something they could lean on in their battles against the effete liberals at home. Deprived of it, they lost their footing.[13]

The swift demise of the Soviet Union was in some ways a sucker punch for this segment of the Right. But it was not long before they regained their footing, arguing that they had been correct all along. It was the tough stance that they had advocated that was alone responsible for bringing the Soviet Union to its knees. Having once criticized Reagan as succumbing to disastrous

12. Heilbrunn, *They Knew They Were Right*, chapter 3.

13. Ibid.

appeasement, they would later recast "Reaganite" to mean aggressive, unilateral action in almost all circumstances.

Leading this effort was Irving Kristol, in a tradition that his son William would continue. While Harries advocated for multilateralism in the post-Cold War era, Irving Kristol went in a different, more fundamentally conservative direction driven by an intense, simplistic moralism. For Kristol, the Cold War did not end—it had just begun. He expressed these views in a revealing 1993 essay entitled "My Cold War."

> There is no "after the Cold War" for me. So far from having ended, my cold war has increased in intensity, as sector after sector of American life has been ruthlessly corrupted by the liberal ethos. It is an ethos that aims simultaneously at political and social collectivism on the one hand, and moral anarchy on the other. It cannot win, but it can make us all losers. We have, I do believe, reached a critical turning point in the history of the American democracy. Now that the other "Cold War" is over, the real cold war has begun.[14]

Note his contempt for an expansively defined "liberal ethos." What does this mean? During the Cold War there was clearly a faction of the American intellectual Left that unfortunately was sympathetic to communism (as Kristol himself had been before becoming an anti-Stalinist). But in no way did that comprise the entire Left, nor the center, nor the moderate Right for that matter. Across this spectrum, there was a broad range of opinion as to how best to defend the United States and how to counter Soviet expansion. In "My Cold War," we can clearly see Kristol's aversion to this nuance. There is the correct conservative view and

---

14. Irving Kristol, "My Cold War (April 1, 1993)," *Brad DeLong's Egregious Moderation* (blog), Oct. 4, 2009, http://delong.typepad.com/egregious_moderation/2009/10/irving-kristol-my-cold-war-april-1-1993.html.

the appeasers, the liberals. The tendency is very much toward a binary view: one or the other. Who is a part of the problem causing moral anarchy—indeed, intent on moral anarchy—and who is not? Are you a virtuous conservative or an apostate?

Broadly, the essay captures conservative qualities that we have discussed in previous chapters. It provides a preview of the certainty and the aversion to compromise that is so much a part of the American Right today. For Irving Kristol, it was not just that liberals might be incorrect on "this or that particular topic. No—liberals were wrong, liberals are wrong, because they are liberals. What is wrong with liberalism is liberalism."[15] It was a fight that he would continue, he said, until his death, and that he would pass on to his children and his grandchildren. Moreover, he describes his neoconservative conversion in terms akin to a fundamentalist awakening—"an experience of moral, intellectual, and spiritual liberation"—liberation from doubt. This outlook runs directly counter to Judge Hand's famous phrase that "the spirit of liberty is the spirit that is not too sure that it is right."

And, in the context of foreign affairs, the combination of certain righteousness and the ability to exercise overwhelming military power tends toward the expansive use of that power. For this reason, Jacob Heilbrunn, in his profile of the neoconservative movement, *They Knew They Were Right*, notes that, in terms of the second Iraq war,

> Many observers remain perplexed that the Iraq war ever occurred. But this is looking at it backward. The neoconservatives had been agitating for something on these lines for decades. Indeed, it would have been more surprising if the war had not occurred.[16]

15. Ibid.

16. Heilbrunn, *They Knew They Were Right*, prologue.

In the 1990s, the inklings of this agitation were evident in the first Iraq war. As we noted in chapter 1, President George H. W. Bush strongly favored a multilateral approach that would set a precedent for how the world should respond to international aggression in the post-Cold War era. His decision to drive Saddam Hussein out of Kuwait, but not to enter Iraq and occupy Baghdad, was directly at odds with the neoconservative views of Irving Kristol, William Kristol, Richard Perle, and Paul Wolfowitz. But the energy for invasion and unilateral actions was clearly there. A decade later, many of the same policy advisors who had been spurned by Bush senior would play a key role in making the case that the United States should invade Iraq during the second Bush administration.

Another glimpse of agitation came in 1991 when Wolfowitz, working for Defense Secretary Dick Cheney, tried to come up with a new, grand strategy guaranteeing continued American domination around the world; he drew it up with the help of his aide I. Lewis "Scooter" Libby, whom he had helped climb the Washington escalator of success since his days as a Yale professor.[17] The outcome of this work was a 1992 draft document, the "Defense Planning Guide," which was intended to be a policy statement on America's mission in the post-Cold War era. The document states that what is most important is "the sense that the world order is ultimately backed by the U.S." and that "the United States should be postured to act independently when collective action cannot be orchestrated."[18] This early effort to promote American unilateralism was rebuffed as well.

In 1996, Robert Kagan and William Kristol, following in the tradition of Kristol's father, made the case in the journal *Foreign Affairs* that the United States should assume a much more

---

17. Ibid., chapter 3.

18. "Defense Planning Guide," excerpts from the 1992 draft, US Defense Department, published by *PBS Frontline*, http://www.pbs.org/wgbh/pages/frontline/shows/iraq/etc/wolf.html.

aggressive, expansive military posture. For Kristol and Kagan, American exceptionalism meant exporting democracy through military might as a benevolent global hegemon. The alternative of leading by example was "a policy of cowardice and dishonor."

> Today's lukewarm consensus about America's reduced role in a post-Cold War world is wrong. Conservatives should not accede to it; it is bad for the country and, incidentally, bad for conservatism. Conservatives will not be able to govern America over the long term if they fail to offer a more elevated vision of America's international role. What should that role be? Benevolent global hegemony.[19]

In the article, they argue that the more cautious approach to global affairs taken by George F. Kennan and, in particular, by John Quincy Adams before him, was now quaint and outdated. Nominally, they were advocating the promotion of liberty and democracy with the aid of military might, but it is interesting to note the number of times they point out that the consensus multilateral approach was "bad for conservatism."

> A true conservatism of the heart ought to emphasize both personal and national responsibility, relish the opportunity for national engagement, embrace the possibility of national greatness, and restore a sense of the heroic, which has been sorely lacking from American foreign policy—and from American conservatism—in recent years. Deprived of the support of an elevated patriotism, bereft of the ability to appeal to national honor, conservatives will ultimately fail in their effort to govern America.[20]

---

19. William Kristol and Robert Kagan, "Toward a Neo-Reaganite Foreign Policy," *Foreign Affairs*, July/Aug. 1996, https://www.foreignaffairs.com/articles/1996-07-01/toward-neo-reaganite-foreign-policy.

20. Ibid.

In the article, Kagan and Kristol invert the meaning of American exceptionalism in precisely the way Hayek's insight about conservatives and imperialism would suggest. However misguided they were on liberty, they did intuitively grasp conservatism, noting that an America leading in foreign affairs primarily by example, rather than by force, was indeed bad for conservatives and conservatism. It would be an exaggeration to accuse Kristol and Kagan of complete cynicism with regard to their intent to export democracy and freedom. But it is hard to read their article without noting the parallel to supply-side economics, a theory that is, at best, a blend of shallow idealism and political opportunism and that was promoted vigorously for decades by William Kristol's father, Irving Kristol, who eventually professed that "political effectiveness was the priority," and not "the accounting deficiencies of government," in which he had little interest.[21]

American "Exceptionalism" and the Iraq Invasion

The 1996 *Foreign Affairs* article provided a theoretical template for a unilateral, militarily driven strategy to export freedom and democracy around the world: for the United States to act alone as a global hegemon. But it was just a template. The attacks of September 11 provided an opportunity to put this theory into practice. Though the attacks originated from Al Qaeda, a stateless terrorist network based in Afghanistan, neoconservatives within the Bush administration immediately turned their attention to nation-states, and to Iraq in particular.

---

21. Paul Starr, "Nothing Neo," *New Republic*, Dec. 4, 1995, reposted by Paul Starr, *Princeton University*, https://www.princeton.edu/~starr/tnr-kris.html.

And, though the putative rationale for invading Iraq was the threat of weapons of mass destruction and a connection to Al Qaeda—that is how the war was sold to legislators and a skeptical American public—the underlying rationale was essentially a conservative impulse to act unilaterally and an associated imperialistic impulse to forcibly spread the blessings of democracy and liberty. Although this sounds completely cynical, part of the problem is that it was not entirely cynical. The easy conflation of the threat of a stateless, radical Islamic network with threats from nation-states was driven in part by simple but strong morality. This theme comes up repeatedly in Heilbrunn's comprehensive history of the neoconservative movement.

> Once again, morality was the key, as well as the putative link between Osama and Saddam. "The more one learns about the Iraqi dictator," wrote Kaplan and Kristol, "the clearer it becomes that he epitomizes—no less than Osama bin Laden—sheer malice. ... He is at once a tyrant, an aggressor and, in his own avowed objectives, a threat to civilization." This, of course, could be said about a number of rulers around the world—but that was Kaplan and Kristol's point: the war against Iraq was only the first shot in an extended campaign around the globe to establish freedom and democracy.[22]

This grand vision, and the simplistic moralism from which it was derived, appealed to the conservative sensibility of George W. Bush. By September of 2002, much of the template for US foreign policy that Kristol and Kagan had outlined in 1996 in *Foreign Affairs* was codified in the "National Security Strategy of the United States," which we discussed briefly in chapter 1.

---

22. Heilbrunn, *They Knew They Were Right*, chapter 4.

Nowhere in the document are the words "benevolent hegemony" to be found, but that is basically what the document proposes. In the aftermath of the September 11 attacks, the document declares that "the United States will use this moment of opportunity to extend the benefits of freedom across the globe."[23] Crucial to this strategy is unchallenged US military might that will be deployed unilaterally, if necessary: "We will not hesitate to act alone, if necessary."[24] In President Bush's opening remarks to the document, he concludes by stating that "the United States welcomes our responsibility to lead in this great mission."[25] Upon invading Iraq in the spring of 2003, George W. Bush proved that he was deadly serious.

Of course, many people on the American Right objected strongly to the 2002 "National Security Strategy of the United States" and the idea of unilaterally invading Iraq. Brent Scowcroft, who served as National Security Adviser under President Ford and under the first President Bush, made the simple point in a *Wall Street Journal* op ed that "Saddam's goals have little in common with the terrorists who threaten us, and there is little incentive for him to make common cause with them"; more important, "our pre-eminent security priority—underscored repeatedly by the president—is the war on terrorism. An attack on Iraq at this time would seriously jeopardize, if not destroy, the global counterterrorist campaign we have undertaken."[26] But Scowcroft was out of step with the simple moralism that

---

23. "The National Security Strategy of the United States of America, September 2002," Washington, DC, http://www.state.gov/documents/organization/63562.pdf.

24. Ibid.

25. Ibid.

26. Brent Scowcroft, "Don't Attack Saddam," Commentary, *Wall Street Journal*, Aug. 5, 2002, http://www.wsj.com/articles/SB1029371773228069195.

would soon convert the "war on terrorism" to an even more open-ended "war on terror." Perhaps the most eloquent rebuttal to America's new foreign policy came from Harries:

> In insisting upon the dominant role of the United States and the assertive use of American power, the ["National Security Strategy of the United States"] makes very questionable assumptions about what the other states will accept. They are asked to take good intentions on trust, but states have never been prepared to do this with other would-be hegemons. Will the United States be the exception? Does the fact that it is a democratic and liberal state make a decisive difference? Will other states accept the concept of a benign hegemon or regard it as a contradiction in terms? Bearing in mind the distrust of unbalanced and concentrated power that is manifest in the United States' own constitution, Americans should not be surprised if others are skeptical.[27]

Harries concludes this piece by quoting himself from an essay he had written in the early 1990s on the perils of exporting liberty and democracy by force. It is a passage with a more timeless quality. It stands in sharp contrast to "the coalition of the certain" that was built in part by Irving Kristol and that tends to dominate the American Right today.

> While determination and purposefulness are important ingredients in any effective policy, the attempt to force history in the direction of democracy by an exercise of will is likely to produce more unintended than intended consequences. The successful promotion of democracy calls

---

27. Harries, "The Perils of Hegemony."

for restraint and patience, a sense of limits and an appreciation of the wisdom of indirection, a profound understanding of the particularity of circumstances. As Thomas Carlyle once put it, "I don't pretend to understand the Universe—it's a great deal bigger than I am ... People ought to be modester."[28]

In this way, Harries's approach to foreign policy is at once consistent with the principles of a free society and at odds with the conservative temperament. As stated in the introduction, the more consistently and earnestly one considers the principles required for a free society, the lonelier one tends to be in the GOP today. In addition, the misconception of freedom has a bearing not just on who leads the American Right, but on special interests and their influence over our government—the subject of chapter 5.

---

28. Ibid.

Special Interests
and Free-Market Fundamentalism

In chapters 1–4, we showed how conservatism is better under-stood as a temperament that tends against political freedom. More important, we argued that ideas have consequences: that conflating conservative temperament and the principles of a free society leads to a confused condition wherein conservative sentiment prevails over political freedom. For example, the conservative aversion to legal restraint and the focus on leaders' personalities—having the right people in charge—tends to over-ride the principle that the rule of law should apply equally to all.

We also showed that conservatives and free-market funda-mentalists are not necessarily the same, but there is a reason they often join forces on the Right. The free-market fundamen-talist believes that individuals and private firms freely con-tracting on their own *always* leads to an optimal outcome for society as a whole. They believe the use of a particular item of property affects *only* the interests of its owner. This view dove-tails with conservative aversion to legal restraint, including government regulations. But it also neatly matches the interest of corporations that pollute, commit fraud, or otherwise benefit from weak, ineffective governance.

This chapter focuses on why special interests are such an eager and important partner in promoting free-market funda-mentalism. To be clear, special interests always pose a potential threat to the sound functioning of liberal democracies. But they pose an especially large threat in the United States because they have successfully co-opted the cherished idea of liberty as a way to advance their own interests.

Ironically, free-market fundamentalists often believe they oppose special-interest influence in government. In this chapter, we show just the opposite: how special-interest groups such as the fossil fuel and tobacco industries, which benefit the most from weak and ineffective governance, have been instrumental in promoting and expanding free-market fundamentalism.

* * *

The close connection between powerful corporate special interests and the misguided idealism of free-market fundamentalism first became apparent to me when I was a freshman at Wesleyan University in Middletown, Connecticut, in 1989. I saw an advertisement posted for a "fellowship" in the study of political economy. It was an all-expense-paid trip to the Institute for Humane Studies at George Mason University, in northern Virginia. It provided room and board during a weeklong series of lectures on economics and political liberty. I had nothing but odd jobs lined up for the summer, and I was keen on public policy, political theory, and economics, so I applied and was accepted.

I enjoyed reading the assigned books and texts, but the lectures and discussions were odd. Instructors often interpreted the texts selectively, like a biblical literalist reads the bible, glossing over contradictions and extracting the pieces that reinforced a particular world view. This view was free-market fundamentalism: "the best government is the least government." Indoctrination may be too strong a word, but it was quite clear that the seminars' purpose was to prepare the program's fellows to become ambassadors for "liberty" and to spread the word in our professional careers as "second-hand dealers in ideas," as instructors described the noble possibility before us. In addition, those running the program made it clear that a network of support, including financial scholarships and access to think-tank internships, would be available to those who continued this line of "scholarly" inquiry. Thankfully, I did not choose this path.

I knew something was amiss, but I didn't see the whole picture. To be clear, some of the program's ideas were sound. The lectures pitched the idea that market forces are powerful and can be underappreciated, which is true. They showed that bad, unintended consequences can result from government intervention in the economy, which can also be true. But from here, the pitch made a grand leap to free-market fundamentalism. Government is always the problem, always the enemy.

For example, prior to the George Mason program I had read Alan Blinder's book *Hard Heads, Soft Hearts: Tough-Minded Economics for a Just Society*. Among other parts, I enjoyed the section on acid rain that argued how reducing sulphur emissions that cause acid rain could be most efficiently accomplished by creating a market for pollution permits and steadily reducing the number of permits for auction each year. This idea, right-of-center though it was at the time, was particularly taboo in the context of the "liberty" seminars. The seminars treated pollution as if it did not exist or, if it did, would simply take care of itself as civilization advanced.

The seminars were similarly hostile to the idea that government has a fundamental role in deterring fraud. Prior to the seminars, I had also carefully read Hayek's *The Road to Serfdom*. I recall striking a particularly raw nerve when I used quotes from that book that directly contradicted the seminars' lessons. From the old underlined paperback copy of *The Road to Serfdom* that I still have, the two most unwelcome quotes may have been 1) on the fact that environmental, health, and labor laws may well be worthwhile and fully compatible with a competitive economy:

Though all such controls of the methods of production impose extra costs (i.e., make it necessary to use more resources to produce a given output), they may be well worth while. To prohibit the use of certain poisonous substances or to require special precautions in their use, to limit working hours or to require certain sanitary arrangements, is fully compatible with the preservation of competition. The only question here is whether in the particular instance the advantages gained are greater than the social costs which they impose.[1]

And 2) on the fact that a market economy requires a government to play a central role in deterring fraud:

Even the most essential prerequisite of [a competitive market economy's] proper functioning, the prevention of fraud and deception (including the exploitation of ignorance), provides a great and by no means yet fully accomplished object of legislative activity.[2]

By the end of the program, it was clear that the curriculum was designed more to help corporations fight regulations than to advance scholarly inquiry and understandings of political freedom. That much I understood. However, I was still mostly unaware of what I had stumbled onto and how the program would ultimately fit into a large, multi-decade effort to change the way people think about government.

* * *

---

1. Hayek, *The Road to Serfdom*, 37.

2. Ibid., 39.

Had I known that the Institute for Humane Studies was generously financed by the Koch brothers, the underlying rationale for the seminars would have been clearer.[3] The more a company is involved in making potentially harmful products, the greater the incentive to promote a "philosophy" maintaining that government regulations will only make things worse and will sacrifice liberty and/or lead to tyranny.

The full expanse of this immensely influential long game has become more apparent thanks to the public release of tobacco company documents in the 1990s and 2000s as well as the efforts of scores of diligent researchers. The Koch brothers have played the most critical role in promoting free-market fundamentalism, but they were not alone. Others, such as RJR and Philip Morris, either followed their example or worked alongside them.

Before the mid 1980s, Charles and David Koch had followed in their industrialist father's footsteps, both in expanding the petrochemical and refining businesses he had started and in dabbling in far-right political affairs. But it was in the late 1980s that their efforts became more organized under their new political director, Richard Fink. Fink sold Charles Koch on a grand plan he set forth in a white paper called "The Structure of Social Change." As noted by Jane Mayer in *Dark Money*, the paper approached the manufacture of political change like any other product.

> As Fink later described it in a talk, it laid out a three-phase takeover of American politics. The first phase required an "investment" in intellectuals whose ideas would serve as the "raw products." The second required an investment

---

3. Mayer, *Dark Money*, chapter 5.

in think tanks that would turn the ideas into marketable policies. And the third phase required the subsidization of "citizens" groups that would, along with "special interests," pressure elected officials to implement the policies.[4]

Charles Koch admired the plan and provided Fink with the resources to begin implementation. In participating in the "liberty" seminars in the summer of 1989, I was supposed to be a part of Fink's first phase: a cog in the production line for the "raw products" of free-market fundamentalism.

A year later, public-relations executives at RJR launched a similar strategy devised by public-relations specialists Tommy Griscom and Tim Hyde. Griscom had been Ronald Reagan's communications director. Hyde, among other jobs, had run the Republican Party in Iowa, an important state for presidential politics. A long memo outlining the strategy for RJR and others became public in 1998 as part of a settlement between the major US tobacco companies and 46 states, five US territories, and the District of Columbia. The memo, titled "Coalitions," was written by Hyde to Griscom:

> You asked for my thoughts on how we might build broad coalitions around the issue-cluster of freedom, choice, and privacy; and what organizations, interests and groups might be engaged in such coalitions. ... First of all, I think coalition-building should proceed along two tracks: a) a grassroots, organizational and largely local track; b) and a national, intellectual track within the DC-New York corridor. Ultimately, we are talking about a "movement," a national effort to change the way people think about government's (and big business') role in our lives. Any such effort requires an

---

4. Ibid., chapter 11.

intellectual foundation—a set of theoretical and ideological arguments on its behalf.[5]

A critical quote from this memo is Hyde's shrewd observation that "I think there is already a strong predisposition on the part of many conservatives to agree with us on our issues, though one that hasn't been very well articulated yet."[6] Hyde intuitively grasped how the conservative aversion to legal restraint and preference for inactive governance fit with free-market fundamentalism and could be channeled to defend tobacco interests under the rubric of promoting freedom.

Tobacco companies such as RJR had two key reasons to launch such ambitious, long-game strategies to change the way Americans thought about regulation and government. First, tobacco executives recognized the threat that regulation posed to their business. Tobacco companies knew their business model relied heavily on fraud and deception: deliberately misleading the public as to whether their products were addictive and caused cancer. They also knew that giving away their products to minors would create "customers for life" once they were addicted, as company documents eventually revealed.[7] Hyde saw the value of framing their defense as a freedom of choice issue even though what they were actually defending was a business model that relied on misrepresenting science and deceiving consumers about their actual choices.

---

5. Tim Hyde, "Coalitions," memo to Tommy Griscom, quoted in Jeff Nesbit, *Poison Tea: How Big Oil and Big Tobacco Invented the Tea Party and Captured the GOP* (New York: Thomas Dunn Books, 2016), chapter 11.

6. Ibid.

7. Jeff Nesbit, *Poison Tea: How Big Oil and Big Tobacco Invented the Tea Party and Captured the GOP* (New York: Thomas Dunn Books, 2016), chapter 14.

Second, RJR already spent heavily on lawyers, lobbyists, and trade groups like the Tobacco Institute. It could afford political investments in broad efforts to "roll back government." Moreover, as the tobacco industry started to lose fights and its reputation suffered, indirect efforts became much more important. In fighting regulation, it helped to hide their agenda behind a seemingly broad coalition, framing it as part of a general effort to "roll back" government.

In his well-researched book, *Poison Tea*, Jeff Nesbit shows how Big Tobacco executives increasingly relied on general antigovernment campaigns to defend their own narrow interests. One of the more successful efforts was RJR's broad, national Get Government Off Our Back campaign, launched in 1994. It aided Newt Gingrich's GOP House takeover and contributed to the anti-government sentiment that emboldened Gingrich to shut down the government in 1995. Despite appearances, RJR was the campaign's driving force.

A February 22, 1995, letter to a state legislator from the head of the Kansas chapter of Get Government Off Our Back is a good example of its reach. Its letterhead lists no less than twenty-nine separate organizations, from family values and justice groups to business and antitax nonprofits. It included the NRA's "CrimeStrike" unit, Traditional Values Coalition, Home School Legal Defense Association, U.S. Term Limits, American Legislative Exchange Council, Competitive Enterprise Institute, and a host of others. RJ Reynolds' name was nowhere to be found on it though the company solely financed the coalition. ... Another campaign document, a backgrounder designed to answer questions about the nature of the coalition, reiterated GGOOB's goal of rolling back regulations at all levels—but did not mention that it was funded by just RJ Reynolds or that it had been formed for the narrow purpose of defending the tobacco industry. Instead, it said that citizens, small businesses, and civic groups had grown weary of "unwarranted government interference" and had spontaneously risen up to fight back. They were furious at Washington and wanted to send a message, it said. "If we don't stop this growth now, the American system could be in danger of collapsing under the weight of big government," it concluded.[8]

What is remarkable here is that, as broad as this campaign was in scope, its purpose was singularly narrow.

> Bear in mind that RJ Reynolds formed the political coalition and funded it in its entirety for the primary purpose of attacking the FDA tobacco rule (and, secondarily, an OSHA investigation around secondhand smoke). That was its real target. RJR created an entire anti-regulation coalition, across dozens of groups in nearly every state in the country, to mask its true intent in attacking this one regulation that threatened its industry.[9]

The Koch brothers' rationale for their long-game strategy to sway American opinion toward free-market fundamentalism was more of a combination of misguided idealism and raw corporate self-interest. It's hard to draw the exact line separating self-deception and cynicism, but the underlying business logic for their political strategy was the same as RJR's. The petrochemical and petroleum-refining operations that have been core to Koch Industries for decades are dirty businesses in the sense

8. Ibid., chapter 13.

9. Ibid.

that they are prone to produce pollution. Today, for example, Koch Industries is not only one of the nation's largest privately held corporations with revenue of approximately $115 billion[10], it is also one of the largest polluters. In 2012, the Environmental Protection Agency's database revealed Koch Industries to be the #1 US producer of toxic waste.[11] Producing 950 million pounds of toxic waste, it topped the list of 8,000 companies required by law to account for their handling of 650 toxic and carcinogenic chemicals spun off by industrial processes.[12] In 2010, the company was rated the #1 air polluter by the Political Economy Research Center at the University of Massachusetts.[13] And, as carefully documented by the political reporter Jane Mayer, during a very heady period of growth from 1980 to 2005 under Charles Koch's leadership, the company amassed a "stunning record of corporate malfeasance" including record fines and indictments related to clean-air and clean-water violations.[14]

To be clear, some businesses that produce popular, useful products are inherently dirty. The industrial processes associated with those products impose costs on others: what Ronald Reagan called "the trespass of pollution." The whole point of well-designed public health and environmental laws is to enable such industries to operate in a way that reasonably limits costs borne by others and reasonably limits risks posed to workers, public health, and the environment. Without such regulation, the owners of polluting businesses benefit from a large, indirect subsidy from those who bear the pollution, health, and environmental costs.

10. Forbes, "America's Largest Companies," (2014) http://www.forbes.com/companies/koch-industries/

11. Mayer, *Dark Money*, chapter 4.

12. Ibid.

13. Ibid.

14. Ibid.

Thus, the practical consequence of free-market fundamentalism for the Koch brothers is to hand them a large indirect subsidy by either pretending that the significant costs borne by others simply do not exist or by arguing that any efforts to curb their indirect subsidy will lead to "tyranny," and therefore should not be pursued. This free-market fundamentalism was the lesson that I was intended to absorb at the Koch brothers-financed "liberty" seminars.

The best way to think about corporate special interests and free-market fundamentalism is as a transaction. On one side stand corporate interests that pollute, commit fraud, or otherwise benefit the most from weak, ineffective governance. On the other side are think tanks, advocacy groups, academics and academic centers, and politicians who collectively peddle free-market fundamentalism and act as the voice of the freedom fraud. Corporate interests can greatly magnify the political influence they buy if they wrap it in the trappings of "independent" groups that supposedly advance the cause of liberty.

The greater the influence of free-market fundamentalism, the more opportunity there is for bad corporate actors to advance their own interests without being accountable for costs they impose on others. And, as these corporations grow, they then have more resources to funnel to an expanding network promoting free-market fundamentalism.

As RJR and Koch Industries met with success in promoting corporate favoritism masked as defending political liberty, other corporations followed. For example, in 1993 Philip Morris agreed to partner with the Koch brothers to create anti-tax front groups to battle new state taxes. The two companies were particularly interested in refined-oil fees on the coasts and excise taxes on cigarettes. They worked in unison through broad campaigns to roll back government in the name of freedom.[15]

---

15. Nesbit, *Poison Tea*, chapter 1.

This early alliance received a huge boost that same year when President Clinton submitted his first budget to Congress. The budget contained a novel idea to price carbon emissions with a BTU tax and begin combating climate change. Jeff Nesbit, then a communications consultant for Koch Industries' primary lobbying group, Citizens for a Sound Economy (CSE), had a front-row seat to the ensuing battle.

When Clinton's budget arrived in Congress, Rich Fink walked into the American Petroleum Institute with a check in hand for several million dollars. That funding, he told API's leadership, was available if they'd match it and allow CSE to take on just the BTU issue in Clinton's budget. API said yes, and the single-minded campaign to target the BTU tax began in earnest. CSE created the content of the relentless attack ads in media in key states, all with an eye toward demonizing the BTU tax. In the end, they only had to flip a single senator—Democratic moderate David Boren, who represented the swing vote on the Senate Finance Committee. CSE took out one full-page ad after another in Oklahoma's daily newspapers to hang the BTU tax around Boren's neck. It worked. Boren capitulated quickly, the BTU tax was pulled from Clinton's first budget, and CSE and the Kochs had their first significant victory on the new political playing field they had created for themselves with help and guidance from Philip Morris and the American Petroleum Institute.[16]

The impact of this significant victory for Koch Industries, Big Tobacco, and API was magnified by the 1994 election, when many House members lost their seats after voting for the budget

---

16. Ibid.

containing the BTU tax. In Washington lore, they had been "BTUed." The election results enhanced the Koch brothers' reputation and provided a template for further political collaboration between fossil fuel and tobacco interests.

Though this victory was consequential, what has most influenced American governance in the past quarter century is that the Koch brothers, in concert with allied industries and sympathetic wealthy donors, have doggedly pursued Richard Fink's vision. They have followed a social-change strategy that, in Charles Koch's words, runs the gamut of influence from "idea creation to policy development to education to grassroots organizations to lobbying to political action."[17] By 2008, the Koch brothers controlled 34 public policy and political organizations, a powerful network dubbed "Kochtopus" by allies and enemies alike.[18]

In the academic sphere, the simplistic, spurious raw material of free-market fundamentalism has not changed from the self-serving propaganda I was supposed to absorb in 1989. But its reach has spread far beyond the beachhead established at the Institute for Humane Studies at George Mason University. Jane Mayer recently reported that she gleaned from an internal list that "the Charles Koch Foundation was subsidizing pro-business, antiregulatory, and antitax programs in 307 different institutions of higher education in America and had plans to expand into 18 more."[19]

The means of disseminating this raw material has also expanded greatly beyond think tanks and advocacy groups. From modest beginnings in 2007 as part of the Sam Adams Alliance, leaders from the Koch brothers' network and an anonymous,

17. Quoted in Mayer, *Dark Money*, chapter 5.

18. Ibid., chapter 7.

19. Ibid., chapter 5.

climate-change-denial funding group called Donor's Trust have expanded the Franklin Center for Government and Public Integrity into a major force in political "reporting" on state-based issues.[20] The organization has moved into the vacuum left by retreating traditional news outlets battered by revenue losses, especially in classified ads. Its product, of course, is not traditional reporting. The Franklin Center's mission statement makes its motives clear: "We offer a megaphone to those with the best free-market, pro-liberty solutions." ...

> Our competitive advantage in moving the needle is our position in the states as a media outlet trusted by all sides of the debate. We're able to communicate directly to the persuadable middle, reaching audiences not normally receptive to the case for these ideas. Our reporting shapes narratives, drives conversations, and lays the foundation for long-term change. We translate theoretical policy into layman's terms and put a human face on the issues.[21]

One hardly needs to read between the lines to understand what is going on. The basic formula here is very similar to RJR's "Get Government Off Our Back" campaign. The "news" sites often claim to be "watchdogs," but they're guarding industry's interests, not the public's. They mix anti-government rancor with themes benefiting large corporate interests, often fossil-fuel energy. For example, some articles question the science of global warming, highlighting the "sprawl" of solar energy or the noise of wind turbines, and urging states to drop out of the clean

20. Nesbit, *Poison Tea*, chapter 20.

21. "About," Franklin Center for Government and Public Integrity, http://franklincenterhq.org/about/.

power plan.[22],[23] They promote the interests of fossil-fuel polluters in the guise of either journalism or pro-liberty advocacy. It's more effective than direct corporate lobbying. That's their "competitive advantage."

In early 2015, Charles Koch said that he and allied donors might spend as much as $889 million to influence the 2016 elections.[24] If all this money came from a single spigot with an overt corporate purpose, its influence on our political system would not be nearly so great. But the sources are so manifold that it's difficult to pinpoint and challenge the spending. The sober reality is that Richard Fink and Charles Koch have significantly influenced our political debate and overall society by persuading important institutions of our liberal democracy —particularly the Republican Party—to accept major elements of their self-serving argument for free-market fundamentalism.

Perhaps they didn't anticipate—or even now fully appreciate—the collateral damage their misguided idealism would do to American governance (a topic that we discuss in chapter 6). But they have been wildly successful in transforming the

22. "Franklin Center for Government and Public Integrity," *Desmog* (blog), http://www.desmogblog.com/franklin-centre-government-and-public-integrity.

23. Suzanne Goldenberg, "Media Campaign against Wind Farms Funded by Anonymous Conservatives," *Guardian*, Feb. 15, 2013, https://web.archive.org/web/20151028234059/http://www.theguardian.com/environment/2013/feb/15/media-campaign-windfarms-conservatives.

24. Matea Gold, "Koch-Backed Network Aims to Spend Nearly $1 Billion in Run-Up to 2016," Politics, *Washington Post*, Jan. 26, 2015, https://www.washingtonpost.com/politics/koch-backed-network-aims-to-spend-nearly-1-billion-on-2016-elections/2015/01/26/77a44654-a513-11e4-a06b-9df2002b86a0_story.html.

politics of environmental law, the area that most directly affects their corporate bottom line. At the end of Ronald Reagan's second term, a sizeable block of Republican legislators had decent records on environmental issues. Today, that block has been eviscerated. The average League of Conservation Voters score for a House Republican now stands at 5 percent, a record low.

Because of the broad, diversified reach of the "Kochtopus" and tacit acceptance on the part of much of the American Right, it's hard to target the push for market fundamentalism at its source. The silver lining is that because free-market fundamentalism is the same simplistic, bad idea I encountered in the Koch brothers-funded "liberty" seminars in 1989, it is not hard to spot. The first step toward reversing the destructive influence of free-market fundamentalism on our governance is to have an easy method to identify it. To do this we can apply a simple "freedom-fraud" test.

Chapter 6

The Freedom-Fraud Test:
#nevertrump, #foreverbachmann?

If politicians, lobbyists, advocates, or citizens promote themselves or a specific proposal by implying it advances freedom, ask three simple questions:

- Do they always portray government as a problem?
- Do they define freedom mainly as the absence of government?
- Are they promoting a principle that applies to many, or to a narrow interest (political, moral, or economic)?

If the answer to the first two questions is yes, then they are using the idea of political freedom to promote something quite different. The answer to the third question, "what is actually being promoted," is usually some combination of conservative temperament and/or corporate special interests.

In our introduction, we noted that the difficult reality about Donald Trump's successful primary candidacy is not the stark break from the conservative movement's idealized version of proper government, but the continuity with the actual behavior of so many conservative activists in recent years. The freedom-fraud test enables us to see this more clearly.

The June 2011 *National Review* cover story on Michele Bachmann provides a good example. Bear in mind that many consider the *National Review* to be *the* magazine for establishment conservatives in the United States, and Robert Costa is a highly regarded conservative writer. As shown on the previous page, the story is titled "Daughter of Liberty" and the cover of the magazine prominently features a radiant Bachmann as a champion of political freedom. By reading the article with the freedom-fraud test's first two questions in mind, we are not as easily snowed. The article portrays her strident stance to repeal legislation and oppose government as assumed proof that she stands for political freedom. But the "tell," as it were, is that it offers nothing substantively about what she has done in government or what she would affirmatively do to promote political freedom. Government is only something to oppose and to indiscriminately roll back.

Stripped of the freedom-fraud veneer, we can see the article for what it is: a mostly fawning portrait of a personality and attitude. It celebrates her refusal to compromise and back down. She is the person who will go to Washington and shake things up. In the article, we also find nostalgia, moralism, and a general affinity for that which is age-old, but nothing serious about the task of governing and the principles of a free society.

Costa quotes Ed Gillespie, the former National Republican Committee chairman, saying Bachmann "has very good instincts about what matters to core Republicans, and she also believes it. ... She is not cowed by the attacks on her by the liberal media and the elite. Plus, on talk radio, on Facebook, and on Twitter, she has a real presence."[1] Without reading too much into Gillespie's comments, it's a bit odd that he feels compelled to emphasize that she actually believes what she says.

The manner in which Costa discusses her personality and

---

1. Robert Costa, "Daughter of Liberty," *National Review,* July 18, 2011

qualifications is telling, too. Costa does point out facets of her personality and career that gave pause to others, and yet he manages to write about these flaws almost as reflections of strength and courage. Here is how Costa describes Bachmann's rise to national recognition:

> When Bachmann opposed the 2008 bank bailouts and Boehner's April 2011 spending deal with Obama, she gave leadership heartburn. She is doing it again this summer with her nonstop push against raising the debt ceiling. But it is Bachmann's Obama barbs, more than anything, that have made her a nationally known name. In October 2008, she appeared on MSNBC and told Chris Matthews that Obama may hold "anti-American views."[2]

Costa offers no evidence from Bachmann as to why she believes Obama is secretly trying to undermine America. And, rather than proceeding to quote perhaps an alternative view as to why such baseless fear-mongering might not be a great idea for a functioning liberal democracy, Costa only states that the GOP establishment was "skeptical of her approach," until "there were murmurs of agreement" online and at rallies and a faucet of small donations started to open and flow. The article describes an establishment catching up to Bachmann, who is in the vanguard of a "freedom" movement.

Costa also manages to present her difficulties working with staff, and her lack of legislative achievements, in a favorable, bucking-the-establishment light.

> Bachmann's congressional office is constantly in flux. She has had six chiefs of staff in her short congressional career,

---

2. Ibid.

and a bushel of press secretaries. Former staffers tell me that she is demanding, press-obsessed, and a scheduler's nightmare. ... "It was impossible," says one former Bachmann aide. "You either get out of her way or you get out of the picture. She does not take disagreement well, and that was fine—that's not unusual in Washington. But she would never listen; she was impulsive. There was a lot of passion, and that was great, but that was the only part of it that was great." The most damning criticism of Bachmann on the Hill, whispered by conservative staffers, is that the House GOP does not have its best face in the presidential field. Bachmann, says one senior GOP aide, is more sales than manufacturing. "I can't think of one bill that she has crafted and passed," he says. Another chortles that her record is a series of television hits. Bachmann's friends contend that she has attempted to do more, only to be blocked.[3]

Again, it's the "chortling" establishment that just does not get it. The article nearly becomes a parody of itself in acknowledging that the "Daughter of Liberty" seemed to lack a basic grasp of American history when she asserted that the Founding Fathers played an integral role in abolishing slavery. The writer acknowledges these deficiencies to avoid complete journalistic malpractice, even as he brushes them aside as only leading to "giggle-giggle stories on the political blogs" and states that her "saving grace may be her sense of humor" that enables her to make light of such gaffes.[4]

In Costa's final analysis, what does Bachmann offer America? In the absence of serious consideration of governance or

3. Ibid.
4. Ibid.

political freedom, there is mostly the residue of the conservative temperament. Foremost, it is the intense focus on personality rather than on the task of governance or the specifics of proposed laws. It is the same quality that Lincoln Chafee described in George W. Bush as so strongly resonating with the conservative base: a person who "will never back down or change course or admit error." For Costa, this is what makes Bachmann a "serious" candidate.

> She is running to change the country, not to make headlines or score a cable-news show. "I know what this will take," she says. "We need someone with a titanium spine who will stand up and repeal Obamacare and turn this country around." ... Bachmann swats away talk of contingency plans. "I believe Obama is highly vulnerable, that he will be a one-term president," she says. "I will bring the resolve and the guts we need to have in the White House so that the United States can remain the indispensable nation of the world."

Those on the American Right who are mystified and chagrined by the rise of Donald Trump should ponder the Costa article. Pundits such as Jennifer Rubin and Erick Erickson, who once offered rousing support for Bachmann, but who now oppose Trump, need to ask how the two differ.[5] Trump, like Bachmann,

---

5. David Frum, "Introducing: Joan of Bachmann Watch," *FrumForum* (blog), July 21, 2011, http://www.frumforum.com/introducing-joan-of-bachmann-watch/. RedState treated any criticism of Bachmann's presidential candidacy only as evidence of the intensely biased "leftist" media: "If there's one mission the leftist-media complex must pursue with dogged, rabid determination, it's that NO strong, accomplished conservative woman should ever be allowed to peer above the fox-hole: They must be

began his rise to national political relevance fanning unfounded fears of "otherness," claiming that Barack Obama was not a legitimate US citizen. And today, the list of important similarities between Trump and Bachmann is long, from promoting Islamophobia, to mocking the science of global warming, to fanning unfounded fears about vaccines.[6] In both cases, their political ascent very much resembles David Frum's description in our introduction, where conservative politicians advance by successfully selling petulant grandstanding as principle, all the while deriding as "weaklings and sellouts" those who note the practical limits of government.

The biggest difference between Bachmann and Trump is mostly one of rhetoric. Trump dispenses with the freedom-fraud language and plays more directly to conservative temperament. He talks about "making America great again," "winning," and other appeals to nationalist sentiment without mentioning freedom. Most of all, he appeals to conservative temperament by selling the idea that he has the right personality and the right attitude to take charge and alone solve our problems. As the Republican National Committee Chair Reince Priebus recently observed, "I think people are judging Trump as to whether he is going to go to Washington and shake things up. And that's why he's doing so well."[7]

destroyed at all costs." Jennifer Rubin hailed Bachmann's "tenacity" and "strength": "As I have said many times, those expecting Bachmann to crumble under the glare of intense scrutiny are kidding themselves."

6. Annie-Rose Strasser, "The 8 Most Outlandish Moments of Michele Bachmann's Time in Congress," Politics, *Think Progress*, May 29, 2013, http://thinkprogress.org/politics/2013/05/29/2070851/bachmann-controversial-moments/.

7. Melissa Chan, "RNC Chair Says Donald Trump Will Have to 'Answer for' Reported Treatment of Women," Election 2016, *Fortune*, May 15, 2016, http://fortune.com/2016/05/15/priebus-trump-treatment-women/.

Understanding that conservative voters value personality and temperament more than true political freedom helps explain Trump's seemingly fast rise and appeal on the American Right. Just five years after the *National Review* published its "Daughter of Liberty" cover story on Bachmann, this same journal published a special, panicky "Against Trump" issue in an unsuccessful bid to derail his primary candidacy. But the underlying reality is that much of the American Right, including many of the editors named in the "Against Trump" issue, had been fanning the flames of conservative temperament at the expense of liberal principles for more than a decade. This brand of conservatism has been increasingly evident with the Right's lack of concern for civil liberties and the rule of law, unserious budget plans that lead to permanent deficit spending, lack of concern about melding religion and politics, the intense focus on the personality of leadership, and a troubled relationship with science, the press, and the empirical world. In this way, the American Right cleared the way; Trump simply came along and dispensed with the freedom-fraud rhetoric.

Erick Erickson of the conservative blog RedState got it right when he observed that the "Republican Party created Donald Trump because they made a lot of promises to their base and never kept them."[8] The critical problem is that the very nature of what much of the American Right has been advocating has been misconception and contradiction, which is why the promises have not been kept.

Trump's success in 2016, if nothing else, exposes how the Republican Party has coalesced around conservative temperament, not around political freedom. Indeed, Trump has enabled

8. Francis Wilkinson, "GOP's Broken Promises Led to Donald Trump's Rise," Commentary, *Chicago Tribune*, Feb. 29, 2016, http://www.chicagotribune.com/news/opinion/commentary/ct-republican-party-broken-promises-rubio-trump-20160229-story.html.

a few political writers to grasp this, referring to the Republican Party's id (conservatism by temperament), on the one hand, and its ego—what Ezra Klein calls "principled conservatism"—on the other. Along these lines, Klein observes that "the core truth Trump has laid bare is that Republican voters are powered by a resentful nationalism more than a principled conservatism."[9] In this situation, the "principled conservatism" to which Klein refers means the liberal principles on which the country was founded, which contrast directly with Trump.

In chapter 2, we noted that the more interesting and perhaps critical dividing line in American politics today is not between Democrats and Republicans but between those who actually believe government has a constructive role in advancing the public good and those who primarily grandstand against it. The freedom-fraud test enables us to keep this important distinction in mind. If our government is to work, the Republican Party cannot become simply a large special-interest faction that denies the possibility of a functioning liberal democracy. Fortunately, we are starting to see some more candid recognition of the bitter-end obstructionism of the American Right. Now out of office, John Boehner speaks openly about the House Freedom Caucus as "knuckleheads" and "goofballs" rather than the guardians of a free society they would like us all to believe they are ("I love all these knuckleheads talking about the party of Reagan ... He would be the most moderate Republican elected today.")[10]

9. Ezra Klein, "Donald Trump's Victory Proves Republican Voters Want Resentful Nationalism, Not Principled Conservatism," Policy and Politics, Vox, May 4, 2016, http://www.vox.com/2016/5/4/11586360/donald-trump-conservatism.

10. Ezra Klein, "John Boehner Just Confirmed Everything Liberals Suspect About the Republican Party," Policy and Politics, Vox, April 28,

Unfortunately, we have advanced dangerously far down this path already. The intense factionalism that "serves always to distract the public councils and enfeeble the public administration" is precisely what George Washington in his farewell address warned would "gradually incline the minds of men to seek security and repose in the absolute power of an individual ... on the ruins of public liberty."[11]

In light of Washington's warning, and after years of Congressional approval hovering at record lows below 20%, is the rise of Trump really so surprising?[12] Washington's warning here is not only germane, it is useful. In using the term "public liberty" to describe the threat to liberty posed by weakened institutions—"distracted public councils" and enfeebled "public administration"—he reminds us that government is indispensable to a free society and that vibrant, active governance has a critical role to play in promoting liberty. In the final chapter we offer a framework to help us think more constructively about government and freedom.

2016, http://www.vox.com/2016/4/28/11526258/john-boehner-ted-cruz-republicans.

11. Washington, "Washington's Farewell Address 1796."

12. "Congress and the Public," Gallup Historical Trends, *Gallup*, accessed June 8, 2016, http://www.gallup.com/poll/1600/congress-public.aspx.

Chapter 7

Recovery: Principles Matter

There has never been a time when liberal ideals were fully realized and when liberalism did not look forward to further improvement of institutions. —*F. A.* **Hayek**

This book began by drawing the broad parallel between the misguided idealism of the far Left in the early part of the twentieth century and the American Right today. We noted that the earnest soul-searching by some on the American Right starting in the 2000s resembled that of the Left from a bygone era. Common to both was a simple question: how did we unwittingly produce "the very opposite of what we have been striving for?" We are now better positioned to understand the parallel to the past and how we might begin to recover.

First, I want to be absolutely clear about what this book does not say. My argument for political freedom is certainly not an argument against religion, spirituality, or religiosity per se; it is not an argument against strong moral codes; it is not an argument against the importance of leadership; it is not an argument against having a shared sense of purpose or of national community; and it is not an argument against traditions or an affinity for things past, which we surely all carry.

The essence of political freedom, however, is to set limitations so that we don't confer arbitrary advantage on the particularities of personality, race, religion, morals, traditions, or simply age-old custom in our national community. With its fear of change and greater caution about the unknown, conservative temperament tends to favor known particularities and to be averse to the inherent, attendant uncertainty of outcomes that result from following general principles. In this way, conservatives can be stewards of liberty, but it requires them to check their conservatism with a sincere appreciation for the principles that define political freedom. Conservatism unbound, such as that associated with fundamentalism (secular or religious), has an inherently contentious relationship with political freedom.

The real danger is when conservative temperament is mistakenly associated with *freedom,* and is directed against the very principles and governance that make us a free society. We saw this in:

- **chapter 1**, where political freedom is perverted to mean the *absence* of restraint in favor of a personality or the "right type" of person in charge;

- **chapter 2**, where the "freeligious" conservatives mistakenly assert religiosity or a particular religion as defining American political freedom; and where we mistakenly construe the strong moralism of the "coalition of the certain" as a political principle contributing to a "conservatism of permanent opposition";

- **chapter 3**, where the defense against a perceived threat to moral cohesion is held above scientific understanding and facts that should be common to all, and foundational to our governance; and

- **chapter 4**, where an imperialistic tendency toward ever larger, outwardly directed military power is extolled over the restrained, defensive, strictly civilian-controlled military that should characterize a free society.

In short, associating conservative temperament with political freedom is a grave misconception, a freedom fraud. Because free-market fundamentalism is directed against all government, and therefore virtually all restraints and limits, it functionally ends up in very much the same place. It eventually favors particularities over general principles, most often embracing an individual's arbitrary discretion. This partly explains how a "libertarian" businessman like Peter Thiel ends up supporting Donald Trump. And, as shown in chapter 5, this is why industries that pollute, commit fraud, or otherwise stand to reap unusual benefit from weak, ineffective governance are important and eager partners in promoting free-market fundamentalism. Finally, this is also why the freedom-fraud test discussed in chapter 6 is effective: why habitually linking anti-government rhetoric to freedom is usually subterfuge for promoting the particularities of personality, special interest, and/or culture war.

The first step toward recovery is to acknowledge the above: to reject the misconception that conservative temperament promotes political freedom. This insight needs to be top of mind when large corporations, industry groups, and/or politicians supported by those groups use broad "campaigns for freedom" to promote their own narrow interests. At minimum, we should avoid empowering wolves with the rhetoric of political freedom for which the "lamb" of liberty will suffer dearly.

Once we've knocked down the claim that government is always the problem—and that being "anti-government" is akin to being "pro-freedom"—we can move from defense to offense. The most practical, direct, and honestly principled route to moving beyond the freedom fraud is to emphasize *how active governance does advance freedom.* The Steve LaTourettes of the world could stand their ground more easily if they expressed their moderation and belief in governance as an affirmation of principle, rather than as an implicit sacrifice of principle and loss of freedom. The American Left can play a role here, by defending good government—and its role in advancing our freedom—more forcefully. Modern progressives share some blame for our general susceptibility to the freedom fraud. Contemporary progressives seldom frame their policy priorities in terms of freedom even when they have legitimate grounds to do so. Their general lack of interest in the concept of political liberty makes it easier for others to co-opt the term inappropriately. As a result, across the political spectrum, there is a kind of implicit acceptance of the false idea that active governance reduces freedom.

* * *

The simple framework shown in the chart on the opposite page may help us move beyond this false idea and better understand the broad parallels with the past. The table places various possible government functions into four columns. This table is not meant to be comprehensive. People can reasonably argue about whether a given function belongs in column 1 versus 2, or 2 versus 3. Still, there's utility in this type of analysis.

Hayek's argument in *The Road to Serfdom* was primarily about column 4. Hayek said the trend to nationalize whole industries, and in particular the effort to direct an entire economy from one central point, placed immense power and discretion in the hands of a few individuals. Such central planning requires destroying many of the essential government prerequisites for liberty in column 1. That's why it's impossible to promote freedom by nationalizing industries.

Two pieces of good news. First, aside from a few cases like North Korea or Venezuela, virtually no political forces advocate nationalizing industries or running centrally planned economies, as was the case in the early twentieth century. In this sense, the main danger that prompted Hayek's warning is not a current threat. Second, functions in the two columns where active governance clearly reinforces liberty are also the least costly. Because these functions are critical to a free society and manageable to fund, they comprise an area where progressives and right-center moderates should be able to work together to support active governance—and do so as a matter of principle. We could say much more about this, but our chief aim here is to understand the nature of the critical problem and offer a direction forward.

Possible Roles of Governance			
1	2	3	4
Essential Prerequisites for Liberty	Neighborhood Effects, Free Rider & Monopoly Issues	Social Insurance, Standards & Urban Planning	Industry Nationalizations/ Complete Central Planning
• Rule of Law & Property Rights • Courts & Law Enforcement • Money & Central Banking • Standards (e.g. Internet Protocol) • Prevention of Fraud & Deception • Intellectual Property • Taxation Function	• National Defense • Pollution • Roads & Infrastructure • Municipal Services • Public Health (vaccination) • Public Education • Anti-trust	• Labor Standards • Factory Laws • Product Performance Standards • Coordinating Infrastructure • National Parks & Monuments • Insurable Risks • Welfare & Progressive Taxation. • Social Security • Healthcare	"The Road To Serfdom"
Active Government & Freedom			
Required	Typically Reinforces	Question of Degree	Undermines
Required Resources from Economy			
Insignificant	Very Manageable	Question of Degree	Total

Earlier in this book, we cited Hayek quoting Adam Smith describing services that "though they may be in the highest degree advantageous to a great society, are, however, of such a nature, that the profit could never repay the expense to any individual or small number of individuals," and therefore justifying, in Hayek's words, a "wide and unquestioned field for state activity." In general, these are column-1 and column-2-type tasks for government. We should always scrutinize a government's efficiency, but let's not be shy about defending government's basic roles. In correctly carrying out these tasks, government reinforces liberty and promotes the public good.

The converse is also true. When government fails in these tasks or provides them unevenly, we lack a level playing field —or even a playing field at all—for individuals to freely pursue their own aims. The harm that results from this failure should not be obscured by the fact that a few special interests might benefit. For example, a counterfeit or a fraud who takes advantage of lax government oversight might reap a concentrated gain that, however small, could produce widespread harm. The confidence required for a currency or an entire marketplace is at stake if these activities are left unchecked. Put another way, the tasks here that support a free society will be carried out only if we at least implicitly acknowledge the requirement of common effort as an important principle. This is the nexus between freedom and a sense of public spirit. And, because our economy and our society keep changing, we never perfect these efforts. Liberty requires vigilant, active government.

Our understanding of conservative temperament helps explain why conservatives might mischaracterize or exaggerate Hayek's thesis. A conservative by temperament tends against active governance that does not support his aims, in particular against evenly applied restraints and limits for those whom he deems to be the "right people in charge," as we saw in chapter 1. This explains the attraction of the idea that such limits, and indeed any government activity, undermines "freedom" and becomes a slippery slope to "the road to serfdom." The more potent distillation of this sentiment is free-market fundamentalism. Here, the misguided idealism is not quite the same as that of the political left of the early twentieth century, but the outcome will tend to be the same, as it undermines the institutions and principles that support political freedom. This is how the American Right produced "the very opposite of what it was striving for."

Lastly, consider column 3. Aside from military spending in a time of war (or during unusual military activity in peacetime), column 3 activities can be the most expensive. And today, this is where most federal government money goes. Whether these activities support or undermine freedom is really a question of degree, the character of the laws, and how those laws are enforced. But we should approach these questions with principles in mind and without hysterical dogma.

For starters, we should immediately dispense with the notion that social services per se threaten freedom or a market economy. The question of freedom in the context of the provision of social services relates primarily to whether one group is gaining arbitrary advantage over another and whether there is still a wide sphere for a private market economy to function properly. In this way, a reasonable social safety net, which *any* member of the national community can access in a time of need, is not conferring arbitrary advantage.[1]

---

1. Those on the political Left or Right who consider Hayek to be a kind of rightward bookend as to what type of social services, if any, would be compatible with political freedom should consider the following

We also should approach tax issues with such principles in mind. In theory, progressive taxation *could* be misused to gratuitously punish one group over another, and/or applied in extreme ways. But let's keep this potential danger in perspective. For example, those who object to a relatively stable and modestly progressive tax structure in the name of "liberty," while also defending tax loopholes that benefit a few—such as comparatively low capital-gains rates, the carried-interest income loophole for hedge-fund and private-equity managers, and special deductions for corporate jet travel—don't stand on principled ground.

---

quotes: "Nor is the preservation of competition incompatible with an extensive system of social services—so long as the organization of these services is not designed in such a way as to make competition ineffective over wide fields" (Hayek, *The Road to Serfdom*, 37); Alternatively, "all modern governments have made provision for the indigent, unfortunate, and disabled and have concerned themselves with the questions of health and the dissemination of knowledge. *There is no reason why the volume of these pure service activities should not increase with the general growth of wealth* (my italics). There are common needs that can be satisfied only by collective action and which can be thus provided for without restricting individual liberty. It can hardly be denied that, as we grow richer, that minimum of sustenance which the community has always provided for those not able to look after themselves, and which can be provided outside the market, will gradually rise, or that government may, usefully and without doing any harm, assist or even lead in such endeavors. There is little reason why the government should not also play some role, or even take the initiative, in such areas as social insurance and education, or temporarily subsidize certain experimental developments. Our problem here is not so much the aims as the methods of government action." (Hayek, *The Constitution of Liberty*, 257-58).

* * *

I hope this book provides a better understanding of the American Right as well as the dynamics of American politics at large. Specifically, once we understand the four characteristics of conservative temperament highlighted in chapters 1–4 and how those tendencies are fraudulently promoted as "freedom," we can see how conservatism undermines liberty. We can better appreciate why our liberal democracy is not functioning as we know it should. We can see why a misguided idealism that is habitually against government leads not to government that is limited, but to politics unlimited.

Donald Trump's success in the 2016 Republican primary is merely a symptom of a problem that has been festering for more than a decade. The hallmark of the American Right in the years prior to Trump—a lack of concern for civil liberties and the rule of law, unserious budget plans that lead to permanent deficit spending, lack of concern about melding religion and politics, the intense focus on the personality of leadership, and a troubled relationship with science, the press, and the empirical world—needs to be acknowledged for what it is: a betrayal of principle that is now deeply ingrained in the American Right. Since this book was partly inspired by the insights of F. A. Hayek on conservative temperament, it is perhaps only fitting to end with his observation that we "shall not grow wiser before we learn that much that we have done was very foolish."[2]

Our realization that past efforts have been greatly misdirected by a basic misconception is at once bitter but also salutary since the error itself can be reversed. This process can begin only by making the case for government's legitimate role in

---

2. Hayek, *The Road to Serfdom*, 239.

terms of principle—in terms of freedom—by unapologetically advocating for active governance where it is clearly required. We can neutralize the freedom fraud by invoking liberty in a way that is legitimate. The path to affirming high ideals lies in addressing pragmatic tasks of governance that are immediately before us, and doing so with an earnest appreciation of political freedom.

Index

A

A World Transformed (Bush, G. H. W./Scowcroft), 41

Abramoff, Jack, 8

Adams, John, 86

Adams, John Quincy, 108, 109, 119

Addington, David, 33, 37, 38

Affordable Care Act of 2010, 70–74

Against the Tide (Chafee), xv

Al Qaeda, xii–xiii, 44, 120

alternative science, 93–94

American Petroleum Institute (API), 136

Americans for Prosperity, xvi, 67

Americans for Tax Reform, 23

Americans United for Separation of Church and State, 54–55

Amway, 65

Anti-Ballistic Missile Treaty, 43

API. *See* American Petroleum Institute

Armey, Dick, xiii, 7–8

Ashcroft, John, 33

authoritarianism, 59, 60, 64–65

B

Bachmann, Michele, 142–44, 145n5, 147

    Trump and, 145–46

Bailey, Ronald, 67

Balanced Budget Act of 1997, 6

Bartlett, Bruce, xiii, 13, 29

benevolent hegemony, 119, 122

biblical literalism, 77, 93, 99

Bill of Rights, 48, 83, 100

Blinder, Alan, 127

blogs

> RedState, 145n5

> Sanchez, 91–92

Bloomberg Politics and Purple Insights poll, 25

Boehner, John, 148

Bolton, John, 42, 43

Boren, David, 136

Brandeis Briefs, 88

Brooks, David, xvii, 103–4

Broun, Paul, 95

BTU tax proposal, 136–38

Buckley, William F. Jr., xxi

budget, federal, xviii

> Affordable Care Act effect on, 74

> Balanced Budget Act of 1997, 6

> Commerce Department percentage of, xxvii

> Omnibus Budget Reconciliation Act of 1990, 5–6

> Recovery and Reinvestment Act of 2009, 70, 73

Bush, George H. W., 13, 93

> foreign policy of son contrasted with, 42–44

> on Hussein, 122

> Kuwait invasion response of, 39, 41

> PAYGO adopted under, 5–7

> tax cuts under, xiii

> World War II and, 40

Bush, George W.

> Chafee on, 69, 91

> foreign policy of father contrasted with, 42–44

> Nixon and, 33, 88

> personality of, xv

security and, 30–38

tax cuts under, xvii

Yoo chosen by, 36–37

Bush, Jeb, 17, 18, 54–55

Bush II administration, xii–xv

decision-making process in, 88–90

deficit spending, 6–7

desire for certainty, 91

expansion of executive power in, 30–38

federal spending during, xiii, 7–8

foreign policy during, xiii–xiv

Iraq invasion obsession of, 87–88, 118

Iraq occupation and, 42

Kagan's essay popularity in, 44–45

legal constraints opposition in, 45

neoconservatism influence in, 65–66

previous Republican administrations contrasted with, 88

religious issues during, xiv

Trump Muslim ban proposal and, 31

Bybee, Jay, 33, 36–37

C

carbon dioxide, 98, 103, 136–37

Carson, Ben, 16–17, 46–47

Cassel, Douglas, 36, 38

CATO Institute, 50, 92

Census Bureau, xxvi

Center for Climate Change Communication, 98

central planning, 154, 155, xxiin16

certainty

Affordable Care Act example of, 70–74

Bush II administration desire for, 91

coalition of, 58–68, 123

exceptionalism, imperialism and moral, 107–20

Chafee, Lincoln, xv, xviii, 91, 145

on Bush, George W., 69, 91

Chait, Jonathan, 6–7, 12, 20

Frum compared to, 21

on Levin, 71–72

on Williamson's speech, 15

Charles Koch Foundation, 137

Cheney, Dick, 6, 25, 33, 38

Citizens for a Sound Economy (CSE), 136

Citizens United, 65

classic liberalism, xxi, xxii, 37–38, 49

conservatives alliance with, 30–31, 50–51

Clean Air Act, 102

climate science, 97–104, 138–39

Clinton, Bill, 6, 7

BTU tax proposal, 136–38

Rome Statute signed by, 41–42

Clintoncare, 72

coalition of the certain, 58–68, 123. *See also* certainty; uncertainty

"Coalitions" memo, 130–31

Cold War, 110, 113, 114, 116

Commerce Department, xxvi–xxvii

communism, xi, 30–31

competition

regulation compatibility with, 127–28

social services and, 157n1

compromise

Affordable Care Act and, 70–74

Bachmann's refusal to, 142, 144

conservative animus against, 68–83

otherness and, 106

Reagan's willingness to, 68

conscientiousness, 59, 60

conservatives and conservatism. *See also* Bush II administration; freedom fraud; Hayek, Friedrich A.; temperament, conservative; *specific topics*

    alliance with classic liberals, 30–31, 50–51

    aversion to change in, 59, 60

    compromise animus of, 68–83

    contempt for treaties and international law, 39–45

    empirical world and, 87–96

    federal spending items opposed by, 4

    fiscal restraint viewed by, 5

    freeligious, 51–58

    Hayek's definition of, 59

    increased, 51, 75

    misperception of, 9

    position on unbound, xxi

    principled, xxiv, 148

    reason for big spending of, 2–5

    Sanchez blog on, 91–92

    security threats response from, 25–30

    shock over Trump, xvii

    small government narrative of, 7

    supply-side economics needed by, 13–16

    tendencies against political freedom, xx–xxi, 24

    tendency against constraint, 37–38

    types of, xxii

Constitution, US, xx–xxi, xxix, 32

    article on census, xxvi

    Jefferson on power and, 38

    Muslim ban and, 27–28

Conway, Erik, 99–101

corporate special interests. *See* special interests

Costa, Robert, 142–45, 147

Cruz, Ted, 17, 47, 69
> on Obama, 67
> on refugees, 54–55

CSE. *See* Citizens for a Sound Economy

D

Dark Money (Mayer), 65, 129–30

"Daughter of Liberty," *141*, 142–45, 147

death panels, Affordable Care Act and, 70, 71

Declaration of Independence, 86, 108

defense spending, 19, 24

deficit spending, 3, 15
> Bush II administration, 6–7
> as taxation deferred, 14

DeLay, Tom, 6–7, 15

Democracy in America (Tocqueville), 109–10, 111

democracy promotion, Harries on, 123–24

Democrats
> federal deficit reduction under, 4–5
> percentage rejecting evolution, 93
> 2015-2016 Democratic primary, 54

Department of Energy, xxvi–xxvii

E

economics. *See* supply-side economics

Economist, 26–27

Eisenhower, Dwight, 57

elections
> Koch, C., intention to influence, 139
> 2006, 7
> 2008, xvi
> 2016, 20

empirical world, conservatism and, 87–96

Bush II administration and, 88–90
  evolution example of, 93–94
enhanced interrogation, 36
Enlightenment liberalism, xxi, xxii, 86. *See also* classic liberalism
  empirical world of conservatives at odds with, 89–90
Environmental Protection Agency (EPA), 102, 134
environmental regulation, 98, 102, 134, 139–40
  BTU tax proposal and, 136–37
EPA. *See* Environmental Protection Agency
Erickson, Erick, 145, 147
Esquire, 89
evolution theory, 93–94, 97
exceptionalism, American
  founders and past leaders in light of, 107–10
  Iraq invasion and, 120–24
  liberty in light of, 107–10, 111
  moral certainty, imperialism and, 107–20
executive power, Bush II expansion of, 30–38
extremism, xvi, xx, 75
Exxon, 103

F

factionalism, 149
faith, 95–96
Falwell, Jerry, 63
federal budget. *See* budget, federal
federal deficit. *See also* deficit spending
  Democrats as reducing, 4–5
  Obama viewed as responsible for, 15–16
  Republican administrations increased, 3, 6–7, 15
  Republican spending financed by, 15
  Trump's plan as increasing, 17
federal spending, 2–25

during Bush II administration, xiii, 7–8

conservatives' types of, 4

on defense, 19, 24

future supply-side, 16–25

items opposed by conservatives, 4

Medicare/Social Security percentage of, 4

PAYGO rule for, 5–7

per-capital growth rate of, 2

Republican record of, 2–5

Fein, Bruce, xii–xiii, 31, 37–38, 58

Feingold, Russell, 32

Feldstein, Martin, 11n5

Fink, Richard, 136, 137, 139

white paper, 129–30

FISA, 32

"fiscal conservative," media use of, 20

fiscal constraint, 19, 21

fiscal irresponsibility, 19

tax cuts and, 17

fiscal restraint, 5, 49

focus group, on Trump's Muslim ban proposal, 26–27

Forbes, Steve, 13

Forbes magazine, 63

Ford, Gerald, 2, 88, 122

Foreign Affairs, 118–19, 120, 121

foreign policy. *See also* exceptionalism; imperialism

Adams, John Quincy, on, 108

during Bush II administration, xiii–xiv, 42–44

Harries on restrained, 113, 123–24

McCain, J., rhetoric on, 111

Trump's, 106

founding fathers, xx–xxi, xxiii, 107–10

Fourth Amendment, 32

Fox News, 18, 19, 92, 102
    on Affordable Care Act, 70, 71, 72
Franklin, Benjamin, 107
Franklin Center for Government, 138
Free to Choose (Friedman, M.), 76
freedom, political
    conservativism tendencies against, xx–xxi, 24
    freedom fraud as misconception of, xxiv
    principles defining, 151–52
    restraints as essential to, 48, 83–84
    simplistic notion of, xxix
    Tocqueville on war as endangering, 109
    uncertainty and, 83–84
freedom fraud
    conservative temperament behind, xxiv, 24, 152–53
    element of truth in, 76
    focus group and, 27
    most potent form of, xxiv–xxv, 79
    powerful narrative of, 21–22
    recovery from, 151–60
    special interests and, 96, 135
    susceptibility to, xxviii, 76
    Tea Party and, 67
    test, 141–42, 148
    trap, 82
freeligious conservatives, 51–58
    primaries and, 52–55, 58
free-market fundamentalism, 75, 77–80
    aversion to uncertainty in, 101–2
    funders of, 102–3
    global warming and, 99, 138–39
    liberty rhetoric of, 125, 138
    obscurantism and, 96

special interests and, 96, 125–40
uncertainty and, 101–2
voices of, 102
voters and, 103
free-rider problems, 77
Friedman, Milton, 76
Friedman, Richard, 27
Frist, Bill, 15
Frum, David, xv–xvi, xxviii
    on Affordable Care Act, 70–71
    Chait compared to, 21
    on crisis of followership, 20–21
"Frum, Cocktail Parties, and the Threat of Doubt" (Sanchez), 91–92
Fukuyama, Francis, xiii–xiv
fundamentalism, 64–65. *See also* free-market fundamentalism;
    religious fundamentalism

G

Garfield, James A., 57
Geneva Conventions, 111
George Mason University, 126
Gergen, David, 20
Get Government Off Our Back campaign, 132, 138
Gillespie, Ed, 142
Gingrich, Newt, 132
global warming, 97–100, 102–4
    free-market fundamentalism and, 99, 138–39
    Stern on governance and, 98
Goldsmith, Jack, 33–34, 35, 36–37
    on Bush II administration, 88
    on Kagan's essay, 45
Good Old Party (GOP). *See* Republican Party
Gorbachev, Mikhail, 114–15

Gore, Al, 42

governance
  advocating for active, 159–60
  free-market fundamentalism fit with inactive, 131
  lack of concern over, xvi–xvii
  personality as more important than, xv, 87, 91, 93, 147
  Republican Party difficulty with principles of, xviii–xx
  Stern on global warming and, 98

government
  best equals least view of, 75–83, 96
  chart on functions of, 154–55, 157
  conservative narrative of small, 7
  essential functions of, xxviii, 77–78, 156
  as free market enemy, 127
  Get Government Off Our Back campaign, 132, 138
  Hayek and Smith, Adam, on, 77–78, 156
  more *versus* less, xxvii–xxviii
  Reagan on, xxv, 75–76, 98–99
  Smith, A., on, 77–78
  social services and, 157n1

governorships, Republican Party 2016, xix, xx

Graham, Lindsey, 25, 111

Grayson, Trey, xvi

Great Recession, 14

Green, Graham, 24

Griscom, Tommy, 130–31

Grunwald, Mike, 22–24

Guantanamo, 47

H

Hard Heads, Soft Hearts: Tough-Minded Economics for a Just Society
  (Blinder), 127

Harries, Owen, 113–14, 123–24

Hastert, Dennis, 15

Hayek, Friedrich A., xi, 4, 52, 159

    Armey and, 8

    on conservatism temperament, xxii–xxiii, 1

    conservative critic position of, xxi–xxii

    conservativism defined by, 59

    on imperialism, 105

    on lack of principles, 49

    liberal position of, xxii

    as neglected, xxii

    on obscurantism, 85

    on regulation and competition, 127–28

    Right wing understanding of, 66

    on science and new ideas, 85, 86–87, 94

    on security threat issue, 26

    Smith, Adam quoted by, 77–78, 156

    on social services, 157n1

    on unrealized liberal ideals, 151

Hayes, Rutherford B., 56

hegemony, benevolent, 119, 122

Heilbrunn, Jacob, 65–66, 113, 121

    on Reagan visit to Moscow, 115–16

    on second Iraq war, 117

Helms, Jesse, 42, 45

Heritage Foundation, 20, 72, 113

Hetherington, Marc, 64

Horton, Scott, 33

hostage-taking tactics, 18

House Committee on Science, Space, and Technology, 95

Huckabee, Mike, 54, 55

Hughes, Karen, 89

Huntsman, Jon, 97

Hussein, Saddam, 39, 41, 110, 118

Bush, George H. W., on, 122
Hyde, Tim, 130–31

I

ICC. *See* International Criminal Court
imperialism, 105–24
    benevolent hegemony and, 119, 122
    Hayek on, 105
    moral certainty, exceptionalism and, 107–20
Inhofe, James, 97
Institute for Humane Studies, 126–29, 137
International Criminal Court (ICC), 41, 43
international law
    contempt for treaties and, 39–45
    Kagan's essay against, 44
    Nuremberg trials and, 40
    Trump and Carson defiance of, 46–47
interrogation, 35, 36
Iraq
    first war in, 41, 42, 118
    second war in, 44, 87–88, 117, 118, 120–24
    weapons of mass destruction and, 88, 110
ISIS, 46–47
Islam, 54, 57

J

Jackson, Andrew, 56
Jackson, Robert H., 39
Jackson, Robert S., 41
Jefferson, Thomas, 38, 56
Jobs, Steve, 90
Jobs and Growth Tax Relief Reconciliation Act of 2003, 6
Judge Learned Hand, 48, 84, 117

K

Kagan, Robert, 44–45, 118–20, 121

Kaplan, Lawrence F., 121

Kasich, John, 53–54

Kemp, Jack, xiii, 13

Kennan, George F., 115, 119

Kennedy, John Fitzgerald, 112

Keynes, John Maynard, 6, 66–67

Khrushchev, Nikita, 15

Kirkpatrick, Jeane, 114

Klein, Ezra, 148

They Knew They Were Right (Heilbrunn), 65–66

Koch, Charles, 62–63, 129, 137
    Fink and, 130
    intended election spending, 139

Koch, David, 129

Koch Industries
    BTU tax opposition success of, 136–37
    EPA on, 134
    rationale for strategy of, 133–34

"Kochtopus," 137

Krauthammer, Charles, 43, 102

Kristol, Irving, 116–17, 118, 120, 121
    Harries and, 113

Kristol, William, 113, 116, 118–20

Kuwait invasion, 39, 41, 110, 118

Kyoto protocol, 43

L

Labrador, Raul, 81–82

Laffer, Arthur, 10, 14, 16–17

Laffer Curve, 10, 14

LaTourette, Steve, 80–81, 153

League of Conservation Voters, 140
Left, American
    parallels between Right and, 61, 151
    role of, 154
Levin, Yuval, 71–72, 93, 94, 94n14
Libby, I. Lewis "Scooter," 118
liberals and liberalism. *See also* classic liberalism
    conservatism conflict with classic, xxii–xxiii
    Enlightenment, xxi, xxii, 86
    founding fathers and, xxiii
    Hayek on, 151
    openness of, 59–60, 61
libertarians, 49–50, 62, 67, 153
liberty
    exceptionalism implications for, 107–10, 111
    free-market fundamentalism rhetoric of, 125, 138
    security threats and loss of, 25–30
    seminars on, 126–29, 130, 135
    spirit of, 117
Lincoln, Abraham, 107, 112
Lindsey, Brink, 50
Lizza, Ryan, 81–82
Locke, John, xxi
Lofgren, Mike, 82, 110–12
Lott, Trent, 15
Luntz, Frank, 26

M

MacArthur, Douglas, 112
Mann, Thomas, xix–xx
Mayer, Jane, 33, 65, 80, 134
    on Charles Koch Foundation, 137
    on Fink's white paper, 129–30

McCain, John, 13, 46, 103, 111

McCain, Stacy, xvii

McKinnon, Mark, 89

media, 20–21, 89, 92

Medicaid, 70

Medicare, 4, 23–24, 70

Merchants of Doubt (Oreskes/Conway), 99–101

military, 107, 109, 111, 117, 122

    civilian control of, 112

moderate Republicans, 80–81, 82

Montreal Protocol, 99

moral convictions

    aversion to uncertainty and, 58–68

    best equals least government, 75–83, 96

    freeligious conservatives, 51–58

    moral certainty, exceptionalism and imperialism, 107–20

    political principles trumped by, 49–84

    presidential primaries and, 52–55, 58

Morris, Philip, 135

Musk, Elon, 61

Muslim ban, Trump's proposed, 25–30, 31

    Washington Post article on, 27–28

N

National Interest, 113

National Religious Liberties Conference, 55

National Review, xvii, 13, 14, 142–45

"National Security Strategy of the United States," 43–44, 121–22, 123

neoconservatism

    Bush II and, 65–66

    military expansion policy of, 109, 117

    Reagan in light of, 114–15

Nesbit, Jeff, 132–33

New Yorker, 33

Nixon, Richard, 3, 33, 88

Norquist, Grover, 18, 22–24, 64–65

Nuremberg trials, 39–40, 41

O

Obama, Barack, 3, 17, 20, 66

    Bachmann's criticism of, 143, 145

    Cruz speech against, 67

    federal deficit associated with, 15–16

    LaTourette meeting after election of, 80–81

    Recovery and Reinvestment Act of 2009, 70

    Trump supporters' ire towards, 27

Obamacare. *See* Affordable Care Act of 2010

obscurantism

    definition of, 87

    funders of, 97, 102–3

    global warming example of, 97–100

    Hayek on, 85

    triad of, 96–104

    voices of, 96, 102

    voter force behind, 97, 103

obstructionism

    bitter-end, 79, 80, 83, 148

    extremism and, 75

Office of Legal Counsel (OLC), 33, 34–35

Omnibus Budget Reconciliation Act of 1990, 5–6

O'Neill, Paul, 87–88, 89

Oreskes, Naomi, 99–101

Ornstein, Norman, xix–xx

otherness, 55, 105–6, 146

P

Paine, Tom, 107

Palin, Sarah, xiv

Patent and Trademark Office, US, xxvi

Paul, Rand, 72–73, 106–7

PAYGO (Pay As You Go), 5–7

Pelosi, Nancy, 15–16

Perle, Richard, 118

Perry, Rick, xxv–xxvi, xxix, 16

personality, of leaders

    Bachmann article highlighting, 142–45

    governance as less important than, xv, 87, 91, 93, 147

    psychology on main traits in human, 59–60

    single leader/single, 90

Pew Research survey, 93

Phillips, Tim, 63

Pigou, A. C., 66

Podhoretz, Norman, 115

Poison Tea (Nesbit), 132–33

Political Economy Research Center, 134

polls

    Pew Research survey on evolution, 93

    on Trump's Muslim ban proposal, 25

pollution, 133–35, 136–37

Powell, Colin, 42

power

    expansion of executive, 30–38

    Jefferson on, 38

"Power and Weakness" (Kagan), 44–45

presidential primaries. *See* primaries, Republican

presidents, religion and politics philosophy of former, 55–57

The Price of Loyalty (O'Neill), 87–88, 89

Priebus, Reince, 146

primaries, Republican, 16–19, 45–47
  Democratic primary of 2015-2016 contrasted with, 54
  foreign policy debate in 2015, 106
  religious and moral themes in, 52–55
  Trump's successful, 141, 145, 147–48, 159
  2012, 52–53
principled conservatism, xxiv, 148
principles, political. *See also* freedom, political; moral convictions,
  political principles trumped by
    compromise and, 69
    for freedom fraud recovery, 151–60
    freedom-defining, 151–52
    Hayek on conservatives' lack of, 49
    taxation governed by, 158

Q

The Quiet American (Green), 24

R

Rand, Paul, xvi
Reagan, Ronald, xii, 5, 6, 13, 31, 130
    compromise approach of, 68
    on environmental regulation, 98
    on government, xxv, 75–76, 98–99
    Heilbrunn on Moscow visit of, 115–16
    neoconservatism and, 114–15
    on pollution, 134
    supply-side opponents and, 20
reality distortion field, 90
recession, 14
Recovery and Reinvestment Act of 2009, 70, 73
RedState blog, 145n5, 147
Reed, Ralph, 63

refugees, 54–55

regulation

carbon dioxide, 98, 103, 136–37

competition compatibility with, 127–28

RJR campaign against, 132–33

tobacco, 100–101, 130–33

religion, 30–31, 50–52, 58. *See also* freeligious conservatives

Bush II administration and, xiv

former presidents on, 55–57

security threats and, 28, 53–54

religious fundamentalism, xiv

authoritarianism and, 59, 60, 64–65

Sullivan on, 58

Republican administrations

deficit increase during, 3, 6–7, 15

federal spending record of, 2–5

Republican Party. *See also* primaries, Republican

fiscal irresponsibility and, 17, 19

former name of, xviii

free society ideal of, xviii–xix

Frum on crisis of followership in, 20–21

governance principles and, xviii–xx

governorships of 2016, xix, xx

hope of course correction for, xv–xvi

moderates, 80–81, 82

most conservative elements of, 97–98

Ornstein and Mann assessment of, xix–xx

Palin choice by, xiv

2016 legislative seats of, xix

"Restrain This White House" (Fein), 31

restraint

foreign policy of, 113, 123–24

freedom fraud and, 152

freedom tied to, 48, 83–84

revenue, from tax cuts, 10–12, 13

Reynolds, R. J., 130, 132–33

Right, American. *See also* conservatives and conservatism; Republican Party; *specific topics*

Bush II directional change in, xiv–xv

cause of anxiety on, xviii

Hayek understood by, 66

Hayek viewed by, xxi–xxii

key dividing line, 80

parallels between Left and, 61, 151

science viewed by, 93, 94, 94n14

soul-searching of, xii–xvii

RJR, 130–33, 138

The Road to Serfdom (Hayek), xi, 127–28

changes to cover of, 66, 67

Keynes endorsement of, 66–67

Roberts, Dave, 106

Rome Statute, 41–42

Romney, Mitt, 72

Roosevelt, Theodore, 57

Royal Economic Society, 98

Rubin, Jennifer, 145, 145n5–146n5

Rubio, Marco, 18, 47

rule of law, xii–xiii, 31, 32, 41, 83

Russia, socialist observations in, xi–xii

Ryan, Paul, 25, 30, 52, 71, 72

S

Sam Adams Alliance, 137

San Bernadino attacks, 25–30

Sanchez, Julian, 91–92

Santorum, Rick, 52–53

science
  alternative, 93–94
  climate, 97–104, 138–39
  Hayek on new ideas and, 85, 86–87, 94
  Levin on Right view of, 93, 94, 94n14
  misrepresentation of, 131
  uncertainty and, 100–101
Scowcroft, Brent, 41, 122–23
The Secret of Success (Koch, C.), 63
security threats
  Bush II response, 30–38
  conservatives' response to, 25–30
  religion and, 28, 53–54
seminars, liberty, 126–29, 130, 135
separation of church and state, 52, 54–58
  past presidents on, 55–57
September 11 attacks, 31, 34
  exceptionalism and, 120, 122
  Iraq obsession prior to, 87–88
  unilateralism following, 43–45
Singer, Fred, 100
Sixth Amendment, Bill of Rights, 83
Smith, Adam, 77–78, 156
Social Security, 4
social services, Hayek on, 157n1
socialism, Hayek on, xi, xxii–xxiii, xxiin16
Soros, George, 61, 62, 63
soul-searching, xii–xvii
Soviet Union, 30, 114, 117
  demise of, 115–16
special interests, xxviii
  "coalitions" memo, 130–31
  freedom fraud and, 96, 135

free-market fundamentalism and, 96, 125–40

"Kochtopus" and, 137

liberty seminars and, 126–29, 130, 135

RJR campaign example of, 130–33

Specter, Arlen, 32

spending. *See* federal spending

starving the beast analogy, 12

Stern, Nicholas, 98

"The Structure of Social Change" (Fink), 129–30

Sullivan, Andrew, xiv, 58, 61–62

supply-side economics, 5–6

analogies, 12

conservatives' need for, 13–16

demise of, 16

extreme version of, 10–14, 11n5, 16–17, 24–25

future federal spending with, 16–25

influence of, 9

modest version of, 10, 11n5, 49

Reagan-era opponents of, 20

tax cuts and, 10–16, 11n5

two versions of, 10–13

Suskind, Ron, 92, 95–96

on Bush II administration, 87–88, 89, 91

T

tax cuts

under Bush, George W., xvii

fiscal irresponsibility and, 17

Laffer and, 10, 16–17

Norquist influence and, 23

Norquist's logic supporting, 24

PAYGO and, 5–7

revenue from, 10–12, 13

supply-side economics and, 10–16, 11n5

Trump's plan for, 17

taxation, 79

Clinton's proposed BTU, 136–38

deficit spending as deferred, 14

Jobs and Growth Tax Relief Reconciliation Act of 2003, 6

principled, 158

Tea Party, xvi, 22, 24, 64, 97–98

freedom fraud and, 67

temperament, conservative, xxi, xxiv, 2, 9–10, 26

freedom fraud and, xxiv, 24, 152–53

Hayek on, xxii–xxiii, 1

liberal temperament compared to, 59–60, 61

Muslim ban proposal appeal to, 29

terrorism, 30. *See also* September 11 attacks

war on, 34

Terry, Dennis, 52–53

Tesla Motors, 61

Thatcher, Margaret, xii

They Knew They Were Right (Heilbrunn), 117

Thiel, Peter, 153

Tobacco Institute, 132

tobacco regulation, 100–101

RJR campaign against, 130–33

Tocqueville, Alexis de, 109–10, 111

torture, Yoo's memos on, 34–36

treaties

Anti-Ballistic Missile Treaty, 43

contempt for international law and, 39–45

Kyoto protocol, 43

Rome Statute, 41–42

Truman, Harry, 112

Trump, Donald, xxix

Bachmann and, 145–46
Carson and, 46–47
compromise as scorned by, 69
foreign policy of, 106
hostage-taking tactics of, 18
Muslim ban proposal by, 25–30
successful candidacy of, xvii–xviii, 141, 145, 147–48, 159
supporters' ire towards Obama, 27
tax plan of, 17
Tea Party support of, 24
Turley, Jonathan, 28

U

UN. *See* United Nations
UN Security Council, 42
uncertainty, 59–60
Amway example of discomfort with, 65
authoritarianism and, 59, 60, 64–65
aversion to, 58–68
freedom and, 83–84
rule of law as embracing, 83
science and, 100–101
unilateralism, 18, 41, 43–45.116, 118
exceptionalism and, 120–22
United Nations (UN), 40

V

voters, 140
as free-market fundamentalism force, 103
obscurantism and, 97, 103

W

Walker, Scott, 17

Wall Street Journal, 12–13, 122

Wallis, Jim, 95–96

war

    defensive *vs.* aggressive, 39–40

    "politically correct," 46–47

    on terror, 34, 122–23

    Tocqueville on freedom endangered by, 109

    World War II, 40, 41, 113

Washington, George, 107–8, 109, 112, 149

Washington Monthly, 31

Washington Post, 16–17, 27–28

waterboarding, 36

weapons of mass destruction, 88, 110

Wednesday Group, 23

Weissmann, Jordan, 17

white paper, Fink's, 129–30

"Why I Am Not a Conservative" (Hayek), xxii

Williamson, Kevin, 14, 15–16, 23

    Chait on speech of, 15

Wolfowitz, Paul, 118

World War II, 40, 41, 113

Y

Yanni, Palma, 28

Yoo, John, 33, 34–37, 38

Bibliography

"About." Franklin Center for Government and Public Integrity. http://franklincenterhq.org/about/.

Adams, John Quincy. "She Goes Not Abroad in Search of Monsters to Destroy." July 4, 1821. reprinted by *Repository*, July 4, 2013. http://www.theamericanconservative.com/repository/she-goes-not-abroad-in-search-of-monsters-to-destroy/.

Adams, John. "Argument in Defense of the Soldiers of the Boston Massacre." Boston, MA. December, 1770.

Armey, Dick. "End of the Revolution." *New York Times*, Nov. 9, 2006.

Atkin, Emily. "To Defeat ISIS, Trump Openly Suggests Committing War Crimes." *Think Progress*, Dec. 3, 2015. http://thinkprogress.org/world/2015/12/03/3727303/donald-trump-kill-isis-family-members/.

Banerjee, Neela Lisa Song, and David Hasemyer. "Exxon: The Road Not Taken." *Inside Climate News*, Sept. 16, 2015. http://insideclimatenews.org/content/Exxon-The-Road-Not-Taken.

Bartlett, Bruce. "How Supply-Side Economics Trickled Down." *New York Times*, April 6, 2007. http://www.nytimes.com/2007/04/06/opinion/06bartlett.html?_r=0.

———. Twitter post. Dec. 11, 2015. https://twitter.com/BruceBartlett/status/675408399576756226.

Benen, Steve. "Carson Makes a Rare Endorsement of War Crimes." MaddowBlog. *MSNBC*, Feb. 17, 2015. http://www.msnbc.com/rachel-maddow-show/carson-makes-rare-endorsement-war-crimes.

Benjamin, Alison. "Stern: Climate Change a 'Market Failure.'" *Guardian*, Nov. 29,2007. http://www.theguardian.com/environment/2007/nov/29/climatechange.carbonemissions.

Boston, Rob. "God on the Campaign Trail Months Shy of November,
    Religious Issues Are Already Roiling the 2016 Presidential Elec-
    tion." *Church and State*, Jan. 2016. Featured on *Americans United*.
    https://www.au.org/church-state/january-2016-church-state/
    featured/god-on-the-campaign-trail.

Brooks, David. "The Green Tech Solution." Opinion Pages. *New York
    Times*, Dec. 1, 2015. http://www.nytimes.com/2015/12/01/opinion/
    the-green-tech-solution.html?action=click&pgtype=Homepage
    &clickSource=story-heading&module=opinion-c-col-left-
    region&region=opinion-c-col-left-region&WT.nav=opinion-c-
    col-left-region&_r=1.

Bush, George, and Brent Scowcroft. *A World Transformed: The Col-
    lapse of the Soviet Empire, the Unification of Germany, Tianan-
    men Square, the Gulf War*. New York: Alfred A. Knopf, 1998.

Bush, George W. and Al Gore. *PBS News Hour*. "Presidential Debate."
    Moderated by Jim Lehrer and excerpted by Ray Suarez. Oct. 12,
    2000. http://www.pbs.org/newshour/bb/politics-july-dec00-for-
    policy_10-12/.

"CBS News/New York Times Poll, December 4–8, 2015." Conducted
    by SSRS of Media, PA on behalf of CBS News and the New York
    Times. *CBS News*, Dec. 10, 2015. http://www.cbsnews.com/news/
    poll-donald-trump-top-ted-cruz-second-hillary-clinton-over-
    bernie-sanders/.

Cecil, Hugh. *Conservatism*. London: Home University Library, 1912.
    Quoted in Friedrich A. Hayek. *The Constitution of Liberty*.
    Chicago: University of Chicago Press, 1960.

Chafee, Lincoln. *Against the Tide: How a Compliant Congress Empow-
    ered a Reckless President*. New York: Thomas Dunne Books, 2008.

Chait, Jonathan. "The Facts Are In and Paul Ryan Is Wrong." *New York
    Magazine*, May 10, 2013. http://nymag.com/daily/intelligencer/
    2013/05/facts-are-in-and-paul-ryan-is-wrong.html.

———. "The GOP's Secret Speech." *New Republic*, May 4, 2010. http://
    www.newrepublic.com/blog/jonathan-chait/the-gops-secret-
    speech.

———. *The Big Con: The True Story of How Washington Got Hood-winked and Hijacked by Crackpot Economics*. Boston: Houghton Mifflin Company, 2007.

Chan, Melissa. "RNC Chair Says Donald Trump Will Have to 'Answer for' Reported Treatment of Women." Election 2016. *Fortune*, May 15, 2016. http://fortune.com/2016/05/15/priebus-trump-treatment-women/.

"Congress and the Public." Gallup Historical Trends. *Gallup*. Accessed June 8, 2016. http://www.gallup.com/poll/1600/congress-public.aspx.

Congressional Budget Office. Referenced in "The $900 Billion Slowdown in Federal Health Care Spending." *Committee for a Responsible Federal Budget* (blog), May 6, 2014. http://crfb.org/blogs/900-billion-slowdown-federal-health-care-spending.

Costa, Robert. "Daughter of Liberty." *National Review*, July 18, 2011.

"Defense Planning Guide." Excerpts from the 1992 draft. US Defense Department. Published by *PBS Frontline*. http://www.pbs.org/wgbh/pages/frontline/shows/iraq/etc/wolf.html.

Dreyfuss, Bob. "Grover Norquist: Field Marshal of the Bush Plan." *Nation*, April 26, 2001. http://www.thenation.com/article/grover-norquist-field-marshal-bush-plan/.

Eisenhower, Dwight D. "Speech at Islamic Center of Washington." June 28, 1957. Archived at IIP Digital, *US Embassy*. http://iipdigital.usembassy.gov/st/english/texttrans/2007/06/20070626154822lnkais0.6946985.html#axzz47LFn5STT.

Epstein, Reid J., and Peter Nicholas. "Donald Trump Calls for Ban on Muslim Entry into U.S." *Wall Street Journal*, Dec. 7, 2015. http://www.wsj.com/articles/donald-trump-calls-for-ban-on-muslim-entry-into-u-s-1449526104.

Fein, Bruce. "Restrain This White House." *Washington Monthly*, October 2006. http://www.washingtonmonthly.com/features/2006/0610.fein.html.

Feldstein, Martin. Interviewed by Douglass Clement. *The Region*. July 10, 2006. Posted by Mark Thoma. *Economist's View*. Sept.

20, 2006. http://economistsview.typepad.com/economistsview/
2006/09/an_interview_wi.html.

Ferencz, Benjamin B. "Enabling the International Criminal Court to
Punish Aggression." *Washington University Global Studies Law
Review* 6, no. 3 (2007): 551-566. http://openscholarship.wustl.edu/
cgi/viewcontent.cgi?article=1149&context=law_globalstudies.

———. "Tribute to Nuremberg Prosecutor Jackson." *Pace International
Law Review* 16, no. 2 (2004): 365-375. http://digitalcommons.
pace.edu/cgi/viewcontent.cgi?article=1168&context=pilr.

Fisher, Daniel. "Koch's Laws." *Forbes Online*, Feb. 26, 2007. http://
www.forbes.com/2007/02/26/science-success-management-
lead-ceo-cz_df_0226kochbookreview.html.

"Franklin Center for Government and Public Integrity." *Desmog* (blog).
http://www.desmogblog.com/franklin-centre-government-and-
public-integrity.

Frum, David. "Bored with Governing." *FrumForum* (blog), August
19, 2010. http://www.frumforum.com/bored-with-governing/.

———. "Following Rand Paul to Disaster." *FrumForum* (blog), May 13,
2010. http://www.frumforum.com/following-rand-paul-to-
disaster/.

———. "Introducing: Joan of Bachmann Watch." *FrumForum* (blog),
July 21, 2011. http://www.frumforum.com/introducing-joan-of-
bachmann-watch/.

———. "Wanna Beat Obama? Here's How." *Daily Beast,* Dec. 13, 2012.
http://www.thedailybeast.com/articles/2012/12/13/the-
alternative-to-doomsday-conservatism.html.

———. "Waterloo." *FrumForum* (blog), March 21, 2010. http://www.
frumforum.com/waterloo-page/.

Fukuyama, Francis. *America at the Crossroads: Democracy, Power,
and the Neoconservative Legacy.* New Haven: Yale University
Press, 2006.

Garfield, James A. Speaking on the Sundry Civil Appropriation Bill.
June 22, 1874. *Congressional Record.* 43rd Congress. 1st session.
5384.

"George Soros." *Open Society Foundations.*
https://www.opensocietyfoundations.org/people/george-soros

Gold, Matea. "Koch-Backed Network Aims to Spend Nearly $1 Billion in Run-Up to 2016." Politics. *Washington Post*, Jan. 26, 2015. https://www.washingtonpost.com/politics/koch-backed-network-aims-to-spend-nearly-1-billion-on-2016-elections/ 2015/01/26/77a44654-a513-11e4-a06b-9df2002b86a0_story.html.

Goldenberg, Suzanne. "Media Campaign Against Wind Farms Funded by Anonymous Conservatives." *Guardian*, Feb. 15, 2013. https://web.archive.org/web/20151028234059/http://www.theguardian.com/environment/2013/feb/15/media-campaign-windfarms-conservatives.

Goldsmith, Jack. *The Terror Presidency: Law and Judgment Inside the Bush Administration.* New York: W. W. Norton & Company, 2007.

"Grover Norquist Quotes." *BrainyQuote.* http://www.brainyquote.com/quotes/authors/g/grover_norquist.html.

Grunwald, Michael. "Grover Norquist Isn't Finished." The Agenda. *Politico*, Oct. 21, 2015. http://www.politico.com/agenda/story/2015/10/grover-norquist-tax-interview-000288.

"Gubernatorial and Legislative Party Control of State Government." Ballotpedia. https://ballotpedia.org/Gubernatorial_and_legislative_party_control_of_state_government. (accessed April 12, 2016).

Hand, Learned. "The Spirit of Liberty." Speech delivered at "I Am an American Day." New York, 1944. Edited by Erik Bruun and Jay Crosby. http://www.providenceforum.org/spiritoflibertyspeech.

Harries, Owen. "The Perils of Hegemony." *American Conservative*, June 21, 2004. http://www.theamericanconservative.com/articles/ the-perils-of-hegemony/.

Hayek, Friedrich A. *The Constitution of Liberty.* Chicago: University of Chicago Press, 1960.

———. *The Road to Serfdom: A Classic Warning against the Dangers to Freedom Inherent in Social Planning.* Chicago: University of Chicago Press, 1976.

Hayes, Rutherford B. Opening of 1875 Gubernatorial Campaign speech. Marion, OH, July 31, 1875. Archived by *Rutherford B. Hayes Presidential Center.* http://www.rbhayes. org/hayes/content/files/RBHSpeeches/speech_147_opening_of_the_ gubernatorial_campaign.htm.

Heilbrunn, Jacob. *They Knew They Were Right: The Rise of the Neocons.* New York: Anchor Books, 2009.

"House Science Panel Wears Blinders." Opinion. *Statesman,* Jan. 9, 2013. http://www.statesman.com/news/news/opinion/house-science-panel-sees-no-climate-change/nTrM2/.

Huntsman, Jon. Twitter post. Aug. 18, 2011. https://twitter.com/ JonHuntsman/status/104250677051654144.

Hyde, Tim. "Coalitions." Memo to Tommy Griscom. Quoted in Jeff Nesbit. *Poison Tea: How Big Oil and Big Tobacco Invented the Tea Party and Captured the GOP.* New York: Thomas Dunn Books, 2016. PDF e-book.

Inhofe, James. Interview by Rachel Maddow. *Rachel Maddow Show.* MSNBC. March 15, 2012.

Jackson, Andrew. Letter to the Synod of the Reformed Church. June 12, 1832. *Correspondence of Andrew Jackson,* ed. John Spencer Bassett. Washington, DC: Carnegie Institute of Washington, 1929.

Jacobson, Louis. "Ted Cruz Misfires on Definition of 'Carpet Bombing' in GOP Debate." *Politifact,* Dec. 16, 2015. http://www. politifact.com/truth-o-meter/statements/2015/dec/16/ted-cruz/ted-cruz-misfires-definition-carpet-bombing-gop-de/.

Jefferson, Thomas. "Draft of Kentucky Resolution 1789." Quoted in E.D. Warfield. *The Kentucky Resolutions of 1799* (New York, 1894). 157-58. Quoted in Friedrich A. Hayek. *The Constitution of Liberty* (Chicago: University of Chicago Press, 1960).

———. Letter to Horatio G. Spafford. March 17, 1814. Archived by *Founders Online National Archives.* http://founders.archives. gov/documents/Jefferson/03-07-02-0167.

"John Yoo on torture." YouTube video. 1:06. Posted by "crook-sandliars." Nov. 25, 2008. https://www.youtube.com/watch?v= bO2p0KHyzpw.

Kagan, Robert. "Power and Weakness." *Policy Review* (June and July, 2002): 3-28.

Klein, Ezra. "Donald Trump's Victory Proves Republican Voters Want Resentful Nationalism, Not Principled Conservatism." Policy and Politics. *Vox*, May 4, 2016. http://www.vox.com/2016/5/4/ 11586360/donald-trump-conservatism.

———. "John Boehner Just Confirmed Everything Liberals Suspect about the Republican Party." Policy and Politics. *Vox*, April 28, 2016. http://www.vox.com/2016/4/28/11526258/john-boehner-ted-cruz-republicans.

Krauthammer, Charles. "Obama Operating under His Own Consti-tution, 'Ruling Like A Banana Republic.'" *Real Clear Politics*, June 12, 2014. http://www.realclearpolitics.com/video/2014/ 06/12/krauthammer_obama_operating_under_his_own_ constitution_ruling_like_a_banana_republic.html.

———. "The Bush Doctrine: 'New Unilateralism.'" *Houston Chronicle*, June 8, 2001. http://www.chron.com/opinion/editorials/article/ Krauthammer-The-Bush-doctrine-new-2055304.php.

Kristol, Irving. "My Cold War (April 1, 1993)." *Brad DeLong's Egre-gious Moderation* (blog), Oct. 4, 2009. http://delong.typepad. com/egregious_moderation/2009/10/irving-kristol-my-cold-war-april-1-1993.html.

Kristol, William, and Robert Kagan. "Toward a Neo-Reaganite Foreign Policy." *Foreign Affairs*, July/Aug. 1996. https://www. foreignaffairs.com/articles/1996-07-01/toward-neo-reaganite-foreign-policy.

"Let the Child Live." International Criminal Court. *Economist*, Jan. 25, 2007. http://www.economist.com/node/8599155.

Levin, Yuval. *Imagining the Future: Science and American Democracy.* New York: Encounter Books, 2008. PDF e-book.

Lexington. "Just a Regular Guy: Donald Trump's Supporters Reveal Why They Back Him." *Economist*, Dec. 11, 2015. http://www. economist.com/blogs/democracyinamerica/2015/12/just-regular-guy.

Lindsey, Brink. "Liberaltarians." Commentary. *CATO Institute*http:// www.cato.org/publications/commentary/liberaltarians.

Lizza, Ryan. "A House Divided." *New Yorker*. Dec. 14, 2015.

Lofgren, Mike. *The Party Is Over: How Republicans Went Crazy, Democrats Became Useless, and the Middle Class Got Shafted*. New York: Penguin Books, 2013.

Manier, Jeremy. "Coyne and Levin, Pt. 2." *Science Life* (University of Chicago Medicine and Biological Science), April 9, 2009. https:// sciencelife.uchospitals.edu/2009/04/09/coyne-and-levin-pt-2/.

Mann, Thomas E., and Norman J. Ornstein. *It's Even Worse Than It Looks: How the American Constitutional System Collided with the New Politics of Extremism*. New York: Basic Books, 2013.

Markon, Jerry. "Experts: Trump's Muslim Entry Ban Idea 'Ridiculous,' 'Unconstitutional.'" *Washington Post*, Dec. 7, 2015. https:// www.washingtonpost.com/politics/experts-trumps-muslim-entry-ban-idea-ridiculous-unconsitutional/2015/12/07/ d44a970a-9d47-11e5-bce4-708fe33e3288_story.html.

Mayer, Jane. "The Hidden Power: The Legal Mind behind the White House's War on Terror." *The New Yorker*, July 3, 2006.

———. *Dark Money: The Hidden History of the Billionaires behind the Rise of the Radical Right*. New York: Random House, 2016. PDF e-book.

McConnell, Campbell R. *Economics: Principles, Problems, and Policies* New York: McGraw-Hill Irwin, 2009.

McCormick, John. "Bloomberg Politics Poll: Nearly Two Thirds of Likely GOP Primary Voters Back Trumps Muslim Ban." *Bloomberg*, Dec. 9, 2015. http://www.bloomberg.com/politics/ articles/2015-12-09/bloomberg-politics-poll-trump-muslim-ban-proposal.

Mooney, Chris. *The Republican Brain: The Science of Why They Deny Science—and Reality.* Hoboken, NJ: John Wiley and Sons, 2012. PDF e-book.

Musk, Elon. Interview by Rory Cellon-Jones for *BBC.* YouTube video. 18:17. Posted by "Singularity Videos." Jan. 13, 2016. https://www. youtube.com/watch?v=SB3eYbPWIvE.

National Health Expenditure Accounts (NHEA). "Table 01 National Health Expenditures; Aggregate and Per Capita Amounts, Annual Percent Change and Percent Distribution: Selected Calendar Years 1960-2014." NHE Tables. *Centers for Medicare and Medicaid Services.* Last modified Dec. 3, 2015. https://www.cms. gov/Research-Statistics-Data-and-Systems/Statistics-Trends-and-Reports/NationalHealthExpendData/NationalHealth AccountsHistorical.html.

"The National Security Strategy of the United States of America, September 2002." Washington, DC. http://www.state.gov/ documents/organization/63562.pdf.

Nesbit, Jeff. *Poison Tea: How Big Oil and Big Tobacco Invented the Tea Party and Captured the GOP.* New York: Thomas Dunn Books, 2016. PDF e-book.

"Obscurantism." *Wikipedia.* https://en.wikipedia.org/wiki/ Obscurantism.

Oreskes, Naomi, and Erik M. Conway. *Merchants of Doubt: How a Handful of Scientists Obscured the Truth on Issues from Tobacco Smoke to Global Warming.* New York: Bloomsbury Press, 2010.

Paul, Rand. Interview by Sean Hannity for *Fox News.* Youtube video. 6:04. Posted by "Eduardo89rp." July 24, 2013. https://www. youtube.com/watch?v=O-UiSS7YIrM&feature=youtu.be.

"Public's Views on Human Evolution." Religion and Public Life. *Pew Research Center,* Dec. 30, 2013. http://www.pewforum.org/2013/ 12/30/publics-views-on-human-evolution/?utm_medium=App. net&utm_source=PourOver.

Reagan, Ronald. "Message to the Congress Transmitting the Report of the Council on Environmental Quality." Washington, DC, Oct. 3, 1988.

———. "Inaugural Address." Washington, DC, January 20, 1981.

Roberts, David. "The GOP Is the World's Only Major Climate-Denialist Party. But Why?" Energy and Environment. *Vox*, Dec. 2, 2015. http://www.vox.com/2015/12/2/9836566/republican-climate-denial-why.

———. Twitter post. Dec. 15, 2015. https://twitter.com/drvox/status/676962254416420865.

Roosevelt, Theodore. "Letter to Mr. J. C. Martin Concerning Religion and Politics, November 6, 1908." Published in *Presidential Addresses and State Papers, November 15, 1907, to November 26, 1908*. Vol. 7: 1866-1871.

Rosenberg, Carol. "Rubio: I'd Grow Guantánamo." *Miami Herald*, April 13, 2015. http://www.miamiherald.com/news/nation-world/world/americas/guantanamo/article18449078.html.

Rutz, David. "Charles Koch Responds to 'Dishonest' Harry Reid: 'People Aren't Going to Scare Me Off.'" *Washington Free Beacon*, Nov. 3, 2015. http://freebeacon.com/politics/charles-koch-responds-to-dishonest-harry-reid-people-arent-going-to-scare-me-off/.

Ryan, Paul. "Transcript and Audio: Vice Presidential Debate." *NPR*, Oct. 11, 2012. http://www.npr.org/2012/10/11/162754053/transcript-biden-ryan-vice-presidential-debate.

Saenz, Arlette. "Rick Santorum Disagrees with Pastor's Statement about Non-Christians." *ABC News*, March 19, 2012. http://abcnews.go.com/blogs/politics/2012/03/rick-santorum-doesnt-agree-with-louisiana-pastors-statement-about-non-christians-in-america/.

Sanchez, Julian. "Frum, Cocktail Parties, and the Threat of Doubt." *Julian Sanchez* (blog). March 26, 2010. http://www.juliansanchez.com/2010/03/26/frum-cocktail-parties-and-the-threat-of-doubt/.

"Scientific Consensus: Earth's Climate Is Warming." Global Climate Change: Vital Signs of the Planet. *NASA*. http://climate.nasa.gov/scientific-consensus/.

Scowcroft, Brent. "Don't Attack Saddam." Commentary. *Wall Street Journal*, Aug. 5, 2002. http://www.wsj.com/articles/SB102937 1773228069195.

Starr, Paul. "Nothing Neo." *New Republic*, Dec. 4, 1995. Reposted by Paul Starr. *Princeton University*. https://www.princeton.edu/~starr/tnr-kris.html.

Strasser, Annie-Rose. "The 8 Most Outlandish Moments of Michele Bachmann's Time in Congress." Politics. *Think Progress*, May 29, 2013. http://thinkprogress.org/politics/2013/05/29/2070851/bachmann-controversial-moments/.

Sullivan, Andrew. "The Daily Dish: Leaving the Right." *The Atlantic*, December 1, 2009. http://www.theatlantic.com/daily-dish/archive/2009/12/leaving-the-right/193506/.

———. *The Conservative Soul: Fundamentalism, Freedom, and the Future of the Right*. New York: HarperCollins Publishers, 2006.

Suskind, Ron. "Faith, Certainty and the Presidency of George W. Bush." *New York Times*, Oct.17, 2004. http://www.nytimes.com/2004/10/17/magazine/faith-certainty-and-the-presidency-of-george-w-bush.html?_r=0.

———. *The Price of Loyalty: George W. Bush, the White House, and the Education of Paul O'Neill*. New York: Simon & Schuster, 2004.

Tankersley, Jim. "Arthur Laffer Has a Never-Ending Supply of Supply-Side Plans for GOP." *Washington Post*, April 9, 2015. https://www.washingtonpost.com/business/economy/arthur-laffer-has-a-neverending-supply-of-supply-side-plans-for-gop/2015/04/09/04c61440-dec1-11e4-a1b8-2ed88bc190d2_story.html.

Thoma, Mark. "Per Capita Spending by President." *Economist's View*. Feb. 12, 2013. http://economistsview.typepad.com/economistsview/2013/02/per-capita-government-spending-by-president.html.

Tocqueville, Alexis de. *Democracy in America*, edited by Phillips

Bradley and Francis Bowen. New York: Alfred A. Knopf, 1980. Vol. 2.

"Trump Flexes Fiscal Conservative Creds, But Wants to Stay 'Unpredictable' on Debt Ceiling, Other Key Issues." *Fox News*, Published Oct. 18, 2015. http://www.foxnews.com/politics/ 2015/10/18/trump-flexes-fiscal-conservative-creds-but-wants-to-stay-unpredictable-on-debt0.html.

Uberoi, Namrata, Kenneth Finegold, and Emily Gee. "Health Insurance Coverage and the Affordable Care Act, 2010–2016." Issue Brief. Office of the Assistant Secretary for Planning and Evaluation. US Department of Health and Human Services. March 3, 2016. https://aspe.hhs.gov/sites/default/files/pdf/ 187551/ACA2010-2016.pdf.

Washington, George. "Washington's Farewell Address 1796." Archived by The Avalon Project: Documents in Law, History and Diplomacy. *Yale Law School.* http://avalon.law.yale.edu/ 18th_century/washing.asp.

"WBUR Poll, New Hampshire 2016 Republican Primary, December 6–8, 2015." Conducted by MassINC Polling Group on behalf of WBUR. *WBUR Boston's NPR News Station*, Dec. 11, 2015. http:// www.wbur.org/2015/12/11/donald-trump-new-hampshire-support-climbs.

Weiler, Jonathan, and Marc Hetherington. *Authoritarianism and Polarization in American Politics.* Cambridge, UK: Cambridge University Press, 2009.

Weiler, Jonathan. Audio interview by Chris Mooney for *Point of Inquiry*, Nov. 21, 2011. http://www.pointofinquiry.org/jonathan_ weiler_authoritarians_versus_reality/.

Weisberg, Jacob. "What Today's Republicans Don't Get about Reagan." *New York Times*, Feb. 24, 2016. http://www.nytimes. com/2016/02/24/opinion/what-todays-republicans-dont-get-about-reagan.html?emc=eta1.

Weissmann, Jordan. "A Conservative Group Analyzed Donald Trump's

Tax Plan. The Results are Kind of Hilarious." MoneyBox. *Slate*, Sept. 29, 2015. http://www.slate.com/blogs/moneybox/2015/ 09/29/donald_trump_s_tax_plan_the_tax_foundation_says_ it_would_add_at_least_10.html.

Wilkinson, Francis. "GOP's Broken Promises Led to Donald Trump's Rise." Commentary. *Chicago Tribune*, Feb. 29, 2016. http://www. chicagotribune.com/news/opinion/commentary/ct-republican-party-broken-promises-rubio-trump-20160229-story.html.

Williamson, Kevin. "Goodbye Supply Side." *National Review*, May 3, 2010. http://www.nationalreview.com/article/229574/goodbye-supply-side-kevin-d-williamson.

Zakaria, Fareed, *The Future of Freedom, Illiberal Democracy at Home and Abroad*. New York: W. W. Norton & Company, 2003.

About the Author

Christopher Arndt's first career was as an Equity Analyst and a Partner at Select Equity Group, Inc., a New York-based asset management firm. After contributing to the significant growth of the firm, he left in 2010 to focus on public policy issues, such as accelerating the adoption of clean energy. He was the Director of the New York Chapter of Environmental Entrepreneurs (E2) and currently serves on the board of the NRDC Action Fund. Mr. Arndt attended Wesleyan University where he graduated with honors from the College of Social Studies concentrating in economics, history and political theory. He now lives in Telluride, Colorado with his wife Patty and his two children, Alden and Graham. *The Right's Road to Serfdom* is his first book.